COASTAL & VALLEY WALKS IN SOUTH WALES

COASTAL & VALLEY WALKS IN SOUTH WALES

by
Andrew Johnson

With original drawings
by
Jenny Kirk

LOGASTON PRESS 1992

LOGASTON PRESS
Little Logaston Woonton Almeley
Herefordshire HR3 6QH

First published by Logaston Press 1992

ISBN 1 873827 01 6

Set in Baskerville 10/12 pt by Logaston Press
and printed in Great Britain on Five Seasons 100 per cent
recycled paper by Ebenezer Baylis and Son, Worcester

Contents

Also from Logaston Press

Aspects of Herefordshire, by Andrew Johnson & Stephen Punter
Aspects of Worcestershire, by Andrew Johnson & Stephen Punter
Ludford Bridge and Mortimer's Cross, by Geoffrey Hodges
The Happy Farmers, by Sheila Wenham
The Humble-bee Its Life History and How to Domesticate it, by F.W.L. Sladen
Walks & More, by Andrew Johnson & Stephen Punter
Alfred Watkins A Herefordshire Man, by Ron Shoesmith
Excavations at Hereford's Castle Green, by Ron Shoesmith
Excavations on and close to Hereford's defences, by Ron Shoesmith
The Finds at Hereford, by Ron Shoesmith
Walks in Southern Powys & the Borders, by Andrew Johnson
Is it still raining in Aberfan? by Melanie Doel & Martin Dunkerton
The Burton Court Recipes: English food from Herefordshire, by Helen Simpson

INTRODUCTION

Welcome to 24 coastal and valley walks in South Wales.

Each walk is on definitive footpaths and bridleways with as little road as is compatible to make an accessible walk in each part of the countryside.

All the walks have been walked in the 12 months prior to publication, and comments about awkward fence crossings, or necessary footwear and in one case the option to ford a river have been included in each walk's preamble so that you know what to expect!

The number of the walk relates to the number on the location map. An estimate of the length of time the walk takes is then given. This time only allows for walking at a reasonable pace and not for stopping to admire the view, or to identify all the wayside plants. You'll need to add on extra time for this to suit your own requirements.

There then follows a note about the walk together with some information on the condition of the paths and tracks to be taken. In the descriptions I use 'path' to describe either a well marked route only wide enough to walk along, or where there is no clearly defined route, for example across or alongside fields. 'Track' refers to a well defined wide route, in all probability used by farm vehicles.

Then follows a description of how to reach the walk's start point by vehicle from the nearest town or large village. The symbol on each map indicates the location of the suggested parking place.

The walk itself is then described and the written directions should be read in conjunction with the sketch map provided. I also recommend use of an Ordnance Survey map of the 1:50 000 series to help identify views. The relevant map number and co-ordinates for the start point of each walk are given above the walk's title.

I cannot guarantee that the countryside remains unchanged, so you may find, for example, that some hedgerows have been grubbed up, or that additional fences have been erected and some paths obstructed.

Finally, my thanks go to Jenny Kirk for her drawings and to Steve Wolstencroft for drawing the maps.

LOCATION MAP FOR WALKS

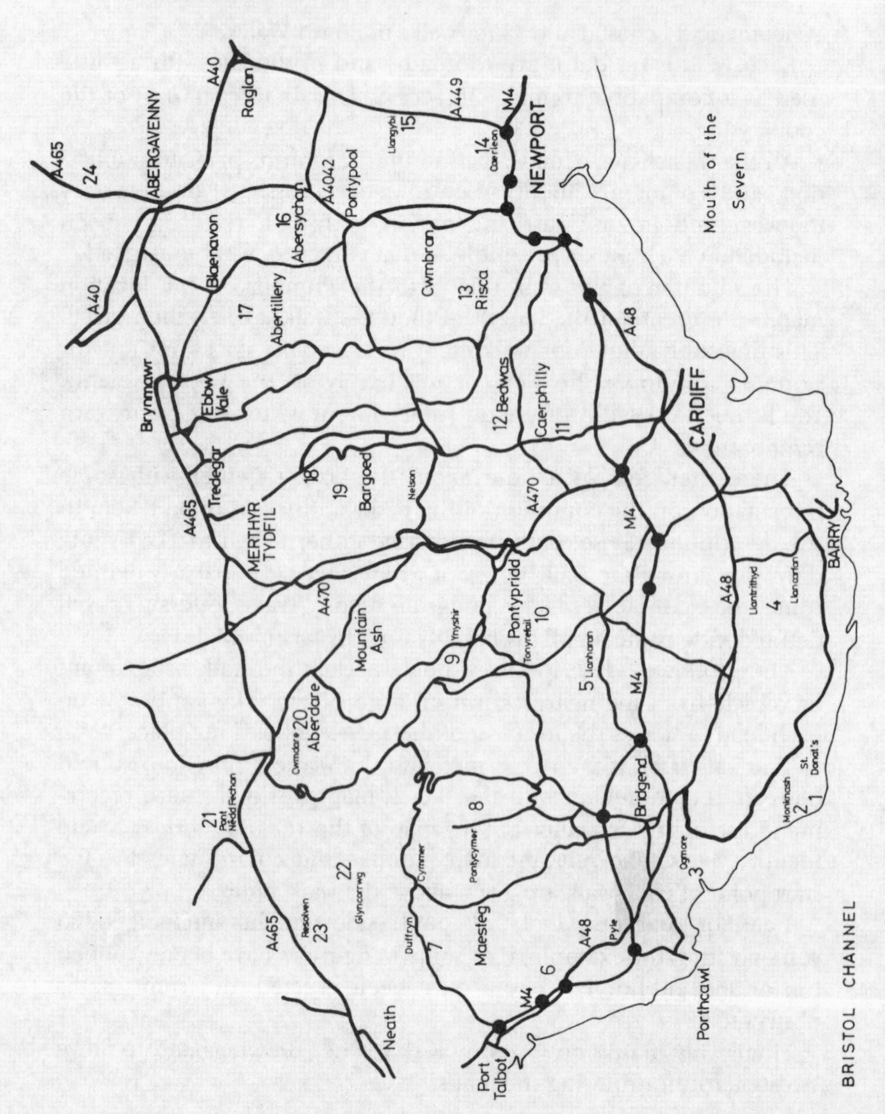

LIST OF WALKS

WALKING LAW AND CODES

General

On a public path the public has a right of access on foot only, and on bridleways a right of access on horse and pedal cycle as well. On each you can take a 'natural accompaniment' which includes a dog, prams and pushchairs. All dogs should be kept under close control, and always on a lead when near livestock. Some public paths are way-marked by the landowner, and have coloured arrows at junctions and changes in direction to indicate the course of the path. The colours are usually yellow for footpaths and blue for bridleways. The highway authority, being the relevant County Council in this area, has a duty to signpost footpaths where they leave a metalled road. There is no time limit in which to fulfill this duty, and in addition signposting can be considered unnecessary in certain limited circumstances. In effect, most paths are neither signposted nor waymarked.

Maintenance

County Councils have a duty 'to assert and protect the rights of the public to the use and enjoyment' of paths and 'to prevent as far as possible the stopping up or obstruction' of such paths. It is normally the surface of the path that belongs to the Council, the soil underneath belonging to the landowner who adjoins the path.

Owners of the land have the primary duty of maintaining stiles, though the Council must contribute a quarter of the cost and can contribute more if they wish.

Often County Councils have agreements with District or Parish Councils whereby the latter maintains the path and charges the County Council; but any complaint about non-signposted, unmaintained or obstructed paths should be sent to the County Council, and can also be sent to the Ramblers Association who may pass it onto a local group to follow up.

Obstructions

If the path crosses a field, the field may be ploughed and planted, but the farmer must make good the surface of the path within two weeks of starting to plough, or if prevented by exceptional weather conditions, as soon as possible thereafter. Reinstatement now has a legal definition under the Rights of Way Act 1990. Minimum widths apply to definitive footpaths and bridleways across and along the edges of fields (1 metre's width is the minimum for a cross field footpath, those for other categories are wider still). Also landowners should remove overhanging vegetation which may inconvenience a walker or prevent the line of the footpath from being apparent on the ground.

If you come across an obstruction on a path, so long as you are a bona fide traveller, in other words if you haven't set out with the specific purpose of removing the obstruction, you're entitled to remove it, but should only remove as much as is necessary to pass through. Alternatively if there is an easy way round the obstruction, you may legally take that route, and would have a defence to any charge of trespass.

Legal action against the landowner lies essentially in the hands of the County Council, and they can prosecute or enter onto the land, carry out the necessary work and reclaim the costs involved. Thus, in case of persistent problems, the information should be passed on to the County Council.

Bulls

It is illegal to keep bulls of a recognized dairy breed (Ayrshire, British Friesian, British Holstein, Dairy Shorthorn, Guernsey, Jersey and Kerry breeds) in fields crossed by a public path, except in open hill areas or if they are under ten months old. Nor is it legal to keep any other bulls in such fields unless accompanied by cows or heifers.

If owners disregard the law relating to bulls and thereby endanger the public, an offence may be committed under the Health and Safety at Work Act 1974, and the police may institute proceedings.

Trespass

If you stray off a path you may be trespassing which is a civil wrong, not a criminal offence, and the landowner may have a remedy in damages and/or an injunction. If you are trespassing solely as a way of avoiding a blockage on a path, then you automatically have a defence.

If you are unsure of your route, remember always to be polite and find out where you should be walking.

Definitive Footpath Maps

The County Council is required to keep a definitive map of footpaths. Ordnance Survey maps may show additional paths and it is these, often still public rights of way, which are most likely to be obstructed or overgrown. It is also more difficult to follow the exact line of paths on the larger scale maps as field boundaries are not shown. Copies of definitive footpath maps can be obtained, usually at a price, from the relevant County Council.

All paths on definitive footpath maps are public rights of way and to show that a path is on such a map is sufficient to establish a legal right of passage. To incorporate paths onto the definitive map it is necessary to prove that the path has been dedicated to public use. This can happen by either act or omission—either the landowner may simply grant the public the right of way, or, alternatively and more likely, you must provide evidence that the public have used the route for at least twenty years without an actual or implied prohibition by the landowner. Applications for additions to the map as well as reports of obstructions should be addressed to the relevant County Council.

Once established a right of way does not 'disappear' simply through lack of use, though this may provide evidence in support of an application to extinguish a path. It is normally the County or District Council who will make an application to extinguish or divert a path, and a publicity and consultation process has to be followed before the order may be confirmed or rejected.

Country Code

Remember when walking to take other peoples' interests in the land into consideration, and remember that you only have the right to walk along the footpaths and not to, for example, use them to carry wood from adjoining land. Remember especially to:

1. Keep any dogs under close control, and you are required to keep a dog on a lead when in a field with livestock. Take additional care at lambing time which normally runs from Christmas to the end of April. If your dog does worry sheep, you may find that not only is it shot, if that is the only way the farmer can stop it, but you may also have to compensate the farmer for any damage it has caused.

2. Leave gates as you find them—remember you may close off livestock from water by closing a gate meant to be open. Always close a gate you've opened to pass through. If it is impossible to open a gate climb over at the hinged end to minimalize the risk of damaging the gate.

3. Always keep to a path unless it is easier to avoid an obstruction by leaving it, which you are entitled to do.

4. Never light fires, and extinguish all matches and cigarettes.

5. Take your litter home.

6. Leave livestock, crops and machinery alone.

7. Make no unnecessary noise.

8. Protect wildlife, plants and trees—remember it may be an offence to damage certain plants and wildlife. It is a simple rule—if you leave them alone they may be there next time for others to see.

Notes on the History of South Wales

The first trace of man in South Wales is a quartzite hand-axe found near Cardiff and which is estimated at 200,000 years old, dating it to an inter-glacial period. It was only by about 10,000 B.C. that people could start to live around the warmer coast as the glaciers made their final retreat, and by 8,000 B.C. evidence that the climate was continuing to warm is given in the remains of carcasses scattered around cooking sites—bones of reindeer and elk giving way to those of red deer, ox and pig. Many of these early sites are now underwater for as glaciers melted with the rise in temperatures, so the sea level rose and man retreated inland before the water.

These early mesolithic inhabitants were soon joined by neolithic peoples travelling over the sea from France and Spain, and by 3,000 B.C. the two had intermingled and formed a more settled existence growing wheat and barley, and raising oxen and pigs.

Other peoples, such as the Celts, joined these inhabitants. Then came the Romans. After their defeat of the Silures and Ordovices on what is now the border of England and Wales, the Romans pushed into South Wales and built the legionary town of Isca, or Caerleon. There are also remains of Roman walls at Cardiff Castle, and those of villas near Cardiff, Llantwit Major and elsewhere in South Wales and in the river valleys further north. However Roman contact with the great hinterland of Wales was minimal.

With the Roman withdrawal to help defend Rome against peoples pressing west from central Europe, the Celtic culture flourished and developed its own spiritual christianity now that it was separated from the church of Rome by pagan Saxons in England. The fifth and sixth centuries saw the great celtic missionary activity of such saints as Cadoc, David and Teilo.

Much of the area covered by this book formed the kingdon of Morgannwg, from which the later name of Glamorgan is derived. For a while in the ninth century this kingdom and much of Wales was united under Rhodri the Great who fought both Danes and Saxons. His grandson Hywel Dda codified Welsh laws and pursued a policy of pragmatic co-operation with the Saxon King Athelstan.

However, once the Normans had subdued England in the eleventh century they instituted their policy of guarding against threats from Wales. Various earldoms were created along the border and given to trusted followers of William I who had come with him to England, with permission that they could conquer what they liked of

Wales and keep it for themselves. Only limited rights over such land were given to the king of England.

William Fitzosborne was created earl of Hereford and was soon moving into Gwent. Later the earls of Gloucester moved into South Wales. The advance of these marcher lords (so-called from the Saxon word mark, meaning border) was briefly halted by Rhys ap Tewdwr of Deheubarth who swore allegiance to William I. But after his death South Wales was overrun and by the reign of Henry I was firmly in Norman hands, though the river valleys extending north and the uplands beyond remained a battlefield for the next 300 years. The Norman overlordship and the return of the church of Rome, meant the end of the Celtic church whose leaders were replaced with aristocratic landowners.

The twelfth and thirteenth centuries saw a swaying of fortunes between the Norman English and Welsh leaders, culminating with the rebellion of Owain Glyndwr in the early 1400's. This rebellion did much destruction to the power of the abbeys; the Wars of the Roses in the latter 1400's saw a marcher lord in the shape of Edward Mortimer become king of England as Edward IV who promptly incorporated much of the marcher powers into that of the crown; and the wars ended with the crowning of a Welshman as king in Henry VII. His son Henry VIII dissolved the weakened monasteries and by selling the lands to ordinary citizens created a whole new middle class in both England and Wales. He also caused the Act of Union between England and Wales, which reorganised Wales into English style administration with shires, and which stated that officers of the crown or state had to be able to speak English.

Wales' culture started to be fused with that of England, but it has always received some encouragement to ensure it is never lost. The Reformation encouraged the bible to be translated into local languages. The Renaissance also encouraged use of native languages, helping Spenser and Shakespeare in England, and the production of a Welsh grammar and dictionary in Wales. But then the 1870 Education Act made English the compulsory medium for primary education in Wales and in the 1890's this was extended to secondary education. However, in 1789 Welshmen in London began to revive the Eisteddfod and in 1791 began the revival of the Gorsedd, the assembly of bards believed to go back to the Druids. More recently education has once again promoted Welsh and Welsh culture.

Know your conifers

Several of the walks pass through or by conifer plantations, and some of the more common species are here briefly described.

Sitka Spruce

The largest spruce, and a native of north-west America, it takes its name from the old Russian capital of Alaska. Naturally coping with sodden ground, and able to withstand high winds, they are grown especially around the high-lying acid boglands. Their wood produces good quality paper pulp, chipboard and sawn timber.

Norway Spruce

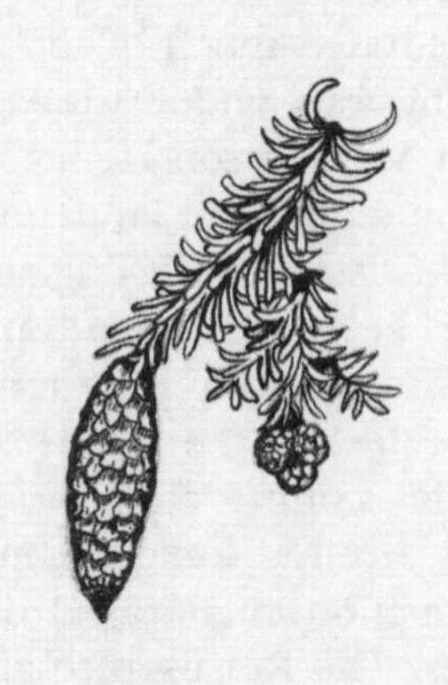

Europe's tallest native tree, reaching 200 feet in height. It has less spiky foliage than the Sitka, and is the Christmas Tree. Originally a native of Britain, but driven south by the Ice Ages, it required importation around 1500 to become re-established. It is more tolerant of frost than the Sitka, but less of acid soil and high winds, so tends to be planted in valley bottoms. Apart from Christmas Trees, it is used as deal or whitewood.

Noble Fir

A native of Canada, it has the largest cone of any tree, with short, tightly clustered needles on the branches.

Lodgepole Pine
This grows at high altitudes in its native area of north-west America, growing at heights of 11,000 feet. Its name is derived from its selection by Indians as the timber support for their wigwams. It is hardy, adaptable and its dense foliage tends to smother competitors, and is well suited to poor, dry soils and exposed sites.

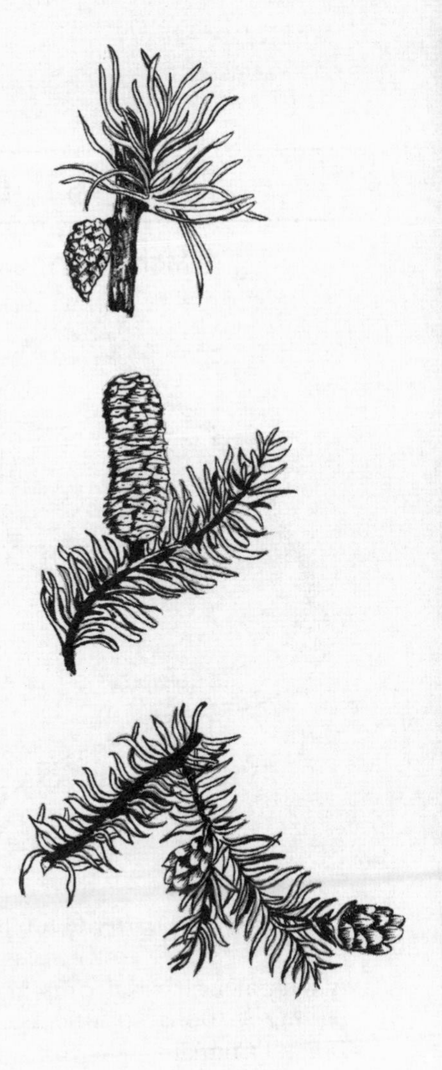

Grand Fir
The largest of the firs, it grows to nearly 300 feet on its native Vancouver Island. It thrives in wet soils.

Western Hemlock
This is different in shape to many conifers, somewhat resembling the native yew in form with its ramshackle drooping branches. It needs constant moisture and so thrives in an environment of perpetual mist and drizzle.

Larch
There are several species of larch, that shown is the Hybrid Larch. The European Larch was introduced into Britain around 1620 and was the predominant tree of timber plantations until it suffered badly from an onslaught of aphids during the mid-nineteenth century. The Japanese Larch was its successor, and by 1904 was being crossed with its European counterpart to produce a faster growing, close grained wood more resistant to insect attack.

ST. DONAT'S

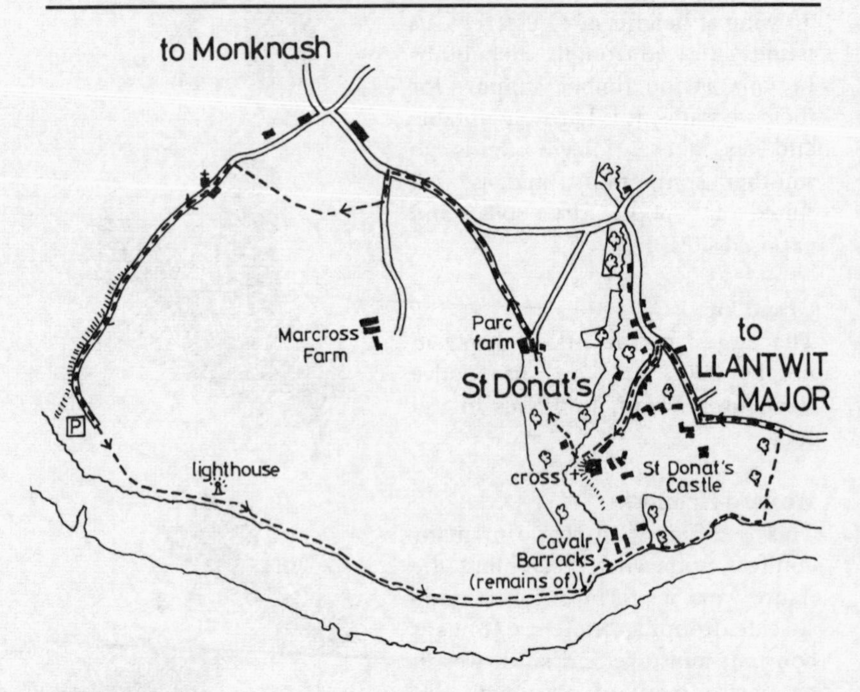

One and three-quarter to two hours.

A walk along coastal cliffs in open fields and gnarled woods, and passing St. Donat's Castle, now a romantic training college, and St. Donat's Church.

From Llantwit Major take the road to St. Donat's. Carry on through St. Donat's and at a staggered crossroads in Marcross just beyond, turn left on the lane signposted to Nash Point and its lighthouse. You can park at the end.

Walk towards the lighthouse, the path then following the road into and round the lighthouse, leaving by the far end over a stone stile. The path then keeps to the field edges along the cliffs, later entering some woodland and passing the remains of old cavalry barracks and it drops down to a little bay. The path continues across the concrete in front of an inshore rescue station, dropping down and up a series of steps. Just past the end of the building go up a few steps on the left, and then up the track back onto the cliff tops. Further on the path divides, but you keep to the left hand path above the cliffs. At the end of the woods the path splits, and you bear left, turning inland away from the sea. You go through one gate and then follow the field boundary on your left to a stile out onto the road.

Turn left on the road, and keep to this past the first entrance to St. Donat's Castle. Turn sharp left at the second entrance just beyond a bend to the left, and walk down the road towards the castle. The footpath then continues to the right of the outer wall of the castle and is signposted to St. Donat's Church. The best view of the castle itself can be had from roughly where this path starts its descent. At the bottom you can visit the church with its gargoyle water spouts and old churchyard cross. Remember also to look up at the castle above you.

From the church walk a few yards back up the lane, turning left onto a track which looks as if it leads to a rubbish tip. Keep right on the track and it will lead you to the right of the remains of an old cottage and then becomes a path through the woodland ahead. When the path splits, keep right and it will lead you out to the right of a farm. Take the left hand lane away from the farm and this will lead you back to the road.

Turn left on the road. When you reach a lane to another farm on the left, take this, but beware as one or two of the paths here are not in the best order and crops may be planted right to field boundaries. If you fancy an easier route, don't take the lane but keep to the road, turning left when you reach the road back to Nash Point.

If walking up the lane, turn right through the first gate you come to, and follow the hedge on your right into the far corner of the field. Here take the gate ahead of you (ignoring the two to your right) and through it once more follow the hedge on your right, soon making a right-angled turn to the right, and then to the left in the next corner. When you reach a gate with supporting stone and block work, go through this and follow the hedge on your right down to some houses, walking out to the road beyond on the lane which circles through them. (It appears the new house here may have been built over the true course of the footpath!)

On the road turn left to return to your vehicle.

MONKNASH

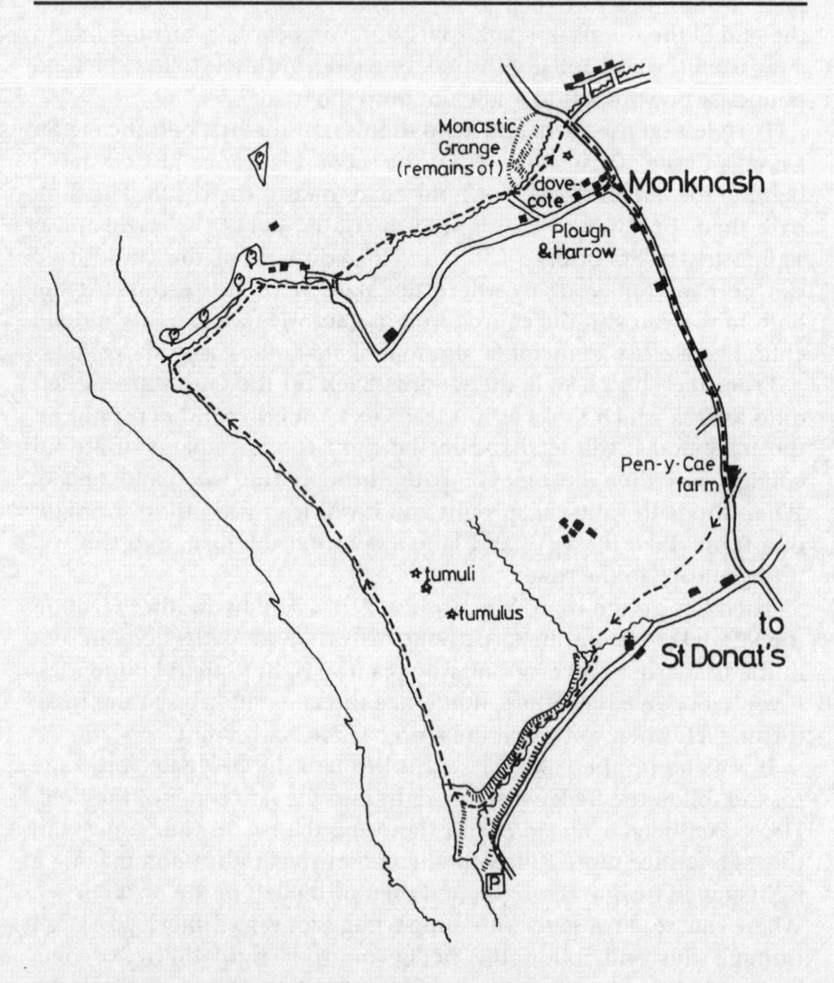

One and three-quarter to two hours.

A walk along cliff tops and the possibility (low tide permitting) of visiting one bay where there is sand to be had, passing the remains of Monknash monastery with its columbarium, and the ability to stop at the pub the Plough and Harrow over half way round. Towards the end you return through a small nature reserve.

From Llantwit Major take the road to St. Donat's. Carry on through St. Donat's and at a staggered crossroads in Marcross just beyond, turn left on the lane signposted to Nash Point and its lighthouse. You can park at the end.

Walk through the gateway on your right as you entered the car park, descending into the valley bottom and then rising between an old fortified headland on the left and the main plateau on your right. The coastal footpath then follows the edge of fields to the next bay, but keep an eye out for three low tumuli on the right hand boundary in the second field (itself enlarged from several smaller ones).

When you reach the next bay there is a sandy stretch at low water of which you may want to make use! The walk itself continues up the cwm on the near side of the stream. The path enters some woodland and then becomes a lane as it nears a stile and gate at the far end. Over the stile turn left, walk over the two stiles to the left of the gate on the driveway to a house, and then take the stile on the right into a field. The path shadows the stream to a stile into the next field, which it crosses cutting off an elbow of the stream. Cross a new stile on the far side and shadow the stream once more to the next stile. In this next field, stay on the nearside of the stream to the top of the field to find the best place to cross the stream, and once over take the stile on your left into the next field. The path now shadows the stream on your left, passing by the left-hand walls of the old monastery buildings with its columbarium or dovecote over to the right. You leave the complex by a gate between a couple of sheds, and find yourself on a road.

Turn right. If you want to visit the pub, bear right at the next junction a few hundred yards ahead. The walk continues along the main road till you reach a farm on your left. Almost opposite a track at the far end of the farm buildings you'll see a stone stile in the hedge on the right. Cross this and walk down the hedge on your right. Just beyond the first field junction off to the right, cross the stile in this hedge, the path now continuing in much the same direction, but following the hedge on your left. In the dingle bottom ahead, cross the stile on your left and then follow the course of the small stream through the field. At the far corner of the field you enter the nature reserve and either of the paths to left or right will lead you through the reserve and back into the area below where you parked.

MERTHYR MAWR & OGMORE

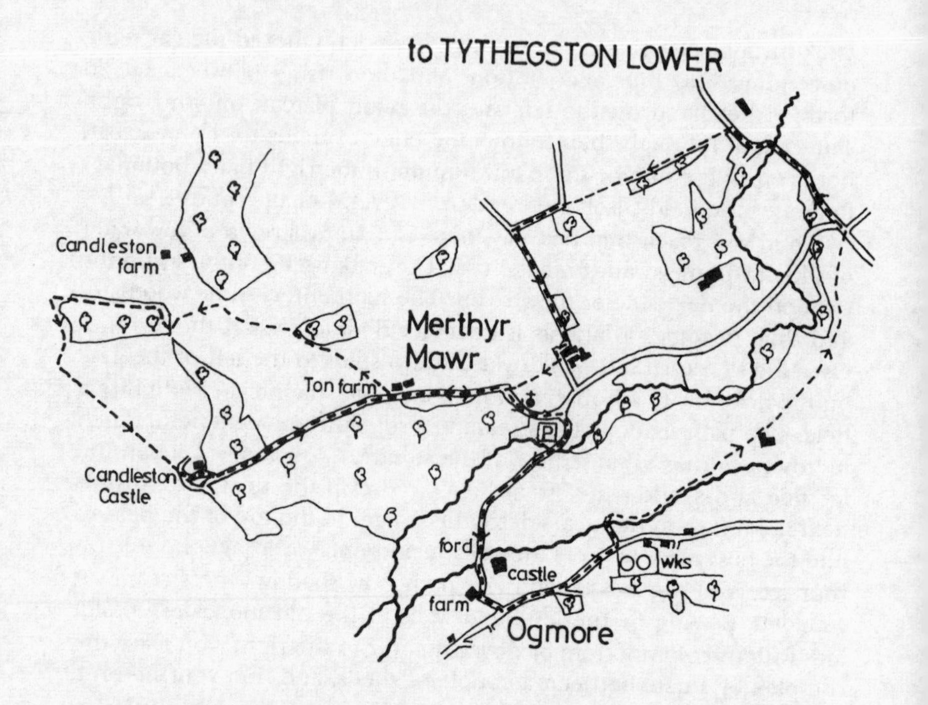

Two and a half hours, though as a walk which is figure of eight shaped it can be broken down into two walks of around one and a quarter hours each.

The circuit to the east includes Ogmore Castle, where there are ruins including much of one wall of the thirteenth century keep and which is reached by stepping stones across the Ewenny River. The walk also includes an old bridge, stone stiles and stone walls. The loop to the west includes sand dunes, some exposed though many overgrown with scrub and grass, with views across the sea and over the Ogmore estuary, together with the remains of the fourteenth century fortified manor of Candleston Castle. Both take in the Somerset-like thatched village of Merthyr Mawr. Each section is on a mixture of mainly paths or minor road.

You want to park in the small car park at Merthyr Mawr by the footbridge across the Ogmore river. Once in the village look out for a track to the left by what look likes a small village green just before you reach the church. This leads to the car park.

For the eastern section leave the car park by the footbridge over the river. For the western section go straight to the paragraph prefaced by *. Once across take the right hand path straight ahead with its concrete surface. This will lead you to the stepping stones and Ogmore Castle. From the castle carry on up the lane to the road at the top. Turn left on this and walk along till you reach a bus shelter on the left. Immediately past this a path leads left and down to a footbridge across the Ewenny. Once over the river turn right and walk along its bank, and you will gradually approach a slight bank above the river, set back from it by some fifty yards. Here you will also be coming into the far corner of a field which is used in a small way as a rubbish dump. Behind this lies a kissing gate and you go through this, and then through the field gate above to enter the field on top of the bank just referred to.

With luck, here you will find a good path maintained through whatever crop is growing. Walk along this which cuts off a corner of field and heads just to the left of the house ahead. Here you cross into the next field and another similar path takes you slightly more to the left and across the next field to a corner of wood on the far side. Go through the gate here and in the next small field follow the now smaller path again slightly more to the left to the internal corner of the field half opposite you, and then here the path turns slightly right and heads for the gate at the far side, to the left of a newer timber-framed house.

Through the gate turn left on the road and go past the turning to the left. Cross the river ahead by the old bridge and round the next bend you'll come to a tarmac drive leading down to the road from the right. Almost opposite where this joins the road, there is another stone stile on your left into the left-hand corner of a field. Go over this stile and then follow the old stone wall on your left all the way along till you cross another stone stile onto another road.

Carry on straight ahead on this road, following it to the left at the bend ahead. If you keep on it it will lead you back to Merthyr Mawr and your car. If you want to include the second loop as well, once the road has made a left bend following almost immediately on one to the right round some barns, cross the stile by a gate into a field on your right, the gate being opposite the entrance to the barns you've just passed around.

Shadow the fence along the field and at the far end of the field pass through the gate onto a path through some woodland to another gate onto a road. Turn right on this.

* If you wish just to walk the western circuit, from the car park walk back up to Merthyr Mawr green and turn left on the road.

On whichever walk you've selected, now follow the road till you reach a fruit farm on your right. As you're passing the last building on your right, go up the short lane which leads to a gate to the field to the immediate left of the farm. Through the gate follow the fence on your right and this will lead you up the hill and over another stile. Here follow the stone wall on your right, starting to diverge slightly from it, aiming for a lone gatepost standing in the middle of the field near the ridge. Here you will join a track which leads downhill and around to a gate out of the field. As you walk down the hill you can see the sandy path you will be taking up the dunes on the far side. Through the gate turn left and follow the field boundary round and then to the left until you come to the sandy path off to your right.

Walk up this and it will head through some scrubby woodland before leading you out onto the open dunes. Once here take the first path you come to on your left. This path presently splits, and the important thing is to keep walking in much the same direction, and trying to stay to the high points. The former means you'll get to see Candleston Castle, the latter that you'll see the sea and estuary!

As you come round the dunes you'll eventually see the overgrown remains of the castle in the valley below you, beyond the foot of a long sand dune slope. After passing the castle, leaving it to your left, you'll meet up with a minor road, and you just follow this back to Merthyr Mawr and the car park.

LLANTRITHYD & LLANCARFAN

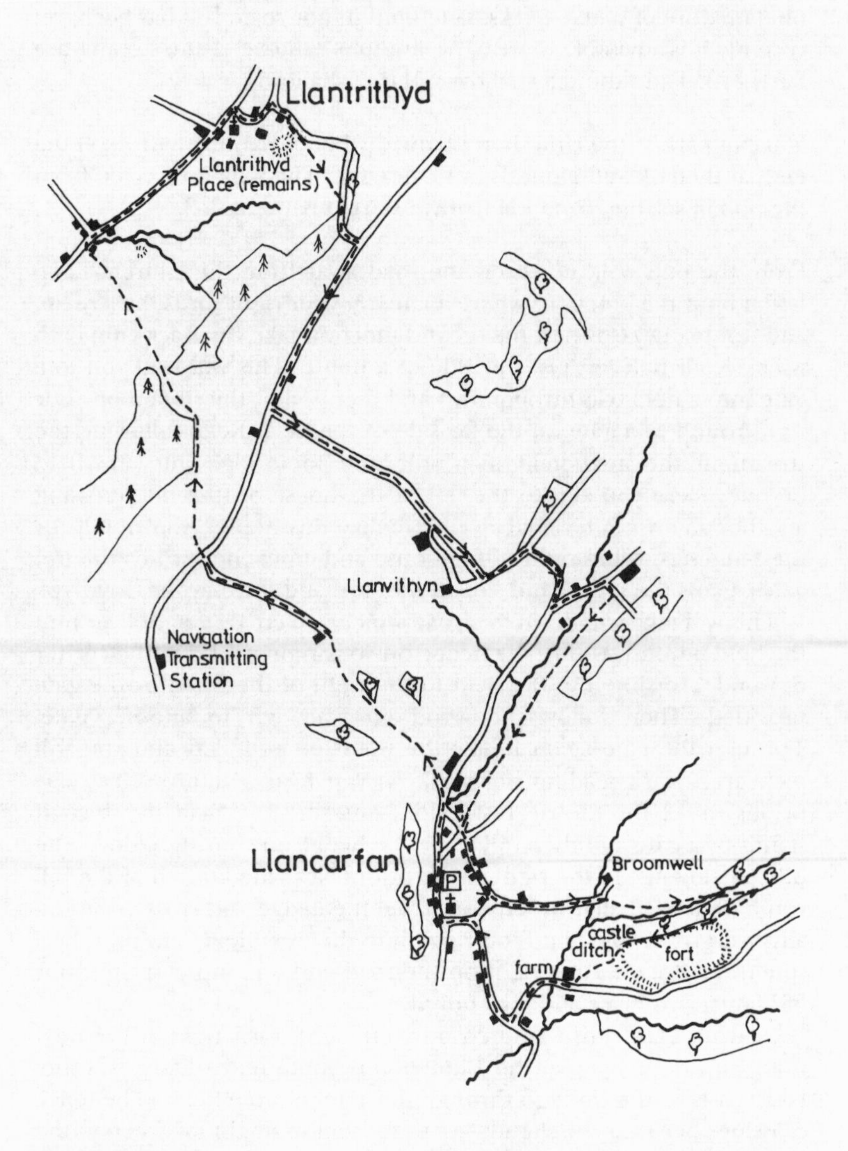

Three hours.

A walk in rolling countryside with several streams and old buildings, including the remains of Llantrithyd Place, near which the church contains a sixteenth century tomb of some of the former owners. There is also a hillfort which the walk half circuits, and the route is on a mixture of paths, tracks, lanes and minor road. If it has been wet recently it is advisable to wear Wellingtons as some of the streams are fairly broad and though shallow, not that shallow!

You can park at the church in Llantrithyd or, if wanting a drink at the end, at the Fox and Hounds in Llancarfan. The walk is directed from the pub; if starting from Llantrithyd start at paragraph 3.

From the pub walk north on the road away from the church. Keep left at both the junctions where a lane on your right fords the stream, and not many yards past the second junction take the track-cum-path which leads half left just this side of a house. This will lead you to a gate into a field. Go through this and then follow the stream on your right round to a gate on the far side of the field. Keep following the stream in the next field to a stile and footbridge into the field beyond. Here you aim to the left of the house on the hill, crossing another stile to enter a steep field below this house. Aim uphill for the buildings to the right of the house and enter the yard by the two gates. Cross the right hand side of the yard and leave by the drive.

This will take you down to a road which you cross straight over into the field beyond. Follow the hedge on your right round to the corner of wood, crossing into the field to the right of the wood by the gate provided. Then follow the wood on your left to another gate. Through the gate again follow the wood on your left and you will pick up a track leading downhill. As you near a line of electricity pylons, head for the nearest pylon, entering the field in which it stands by a gate and then following the hedge on your right down the hill, passing just to the right of the pylon. Near the bottom of the hill you have to veer slightly left away from the hedge and cross a marginally overgrown stile and footbridge into the next field, leaving it by a stile onto a road. Turn right on the road and walk up past the ruins of Llantrithyd Place and the church.

Leaving Llantrithyd Church on your right, turn right at the next road, and right again at the T-junction beyond. Immediately past the last house on the right go through the gate into the field. (The fence crossings here may be slightly awkward, so if in doubt just keep to the road—the two routes will reunite.)

Initially follow the hedge on your left then, when the road bears left, keep on walking on the same line as you were. You cross one field boundary almost immediately and then cross the next field to its far top corner. Here you leave by a stile back onto the road. Turn right on the road, then right again at the T-junction ahead.

Walk along the road till you reach a concrete farm lane off to the left, this side of some barns on the right. Walk down the lane and when you near the farmhouse, take the track which leads round to the left of the house, following this down the hill to join with a lane to another farm. This way one avoids passing too close to either farm, even though it is a diversion from the definitive route. Turn left on the second lane and follow it down to the road, where you turn right.

Follow the road as it bends right, then go through the farm gate a few hundred yards along on the left. Head for the house to the left, taking a route which also doubles back on yourself. Pass below this house on a track, and walk up to the next farm. Here turn right over the stream before you reach the main buildings and enter a field. Turn right to shadow the stream, crossing the first field to a stile in the middle of the far fence. Then follow the hedge on your left and as you approach two new barns below and to your right, walk up into the top left hand corner of the field into some scraggy woodland. Here you'll find a stile onto a path which keeps the same direction and will lead you via more stiles out onto a road. Turn left on the road and cross the road you immediately come to.

When you reach the school on your right, turn left up the lane opposite. Once over a stream, go through the gate on your right. Walk down to the stream and follow it along to the woodland ahead. Here turn right, cross the stream, turn right at the foot of what appears to be a cliff and after only a few yards you come to a slithery narrow path up the bank, suddenly reaching a double stile which you cross. Turn left once over the stiles and walk along to the end of the bank on your right, turning right and walking along the top of it once you reach the end of it. At the far end of the field head up to the top and cross the fence by the stile in the corner. Then turn right and walk along the bottom of the fort's old ditch. Go through the two gates in quick succession where you reach the end of the hill, and once through the second, turn right and follow the fence on your right downhill, emerging onto a road just to the left of an old farm.

Turn right on the road, then left and right at the next junctions to return to the pub. (If starting from Llantrithyd, now start reading from the start of the instructions!)

LLANHARAN & ST. PETER'S CHURCH

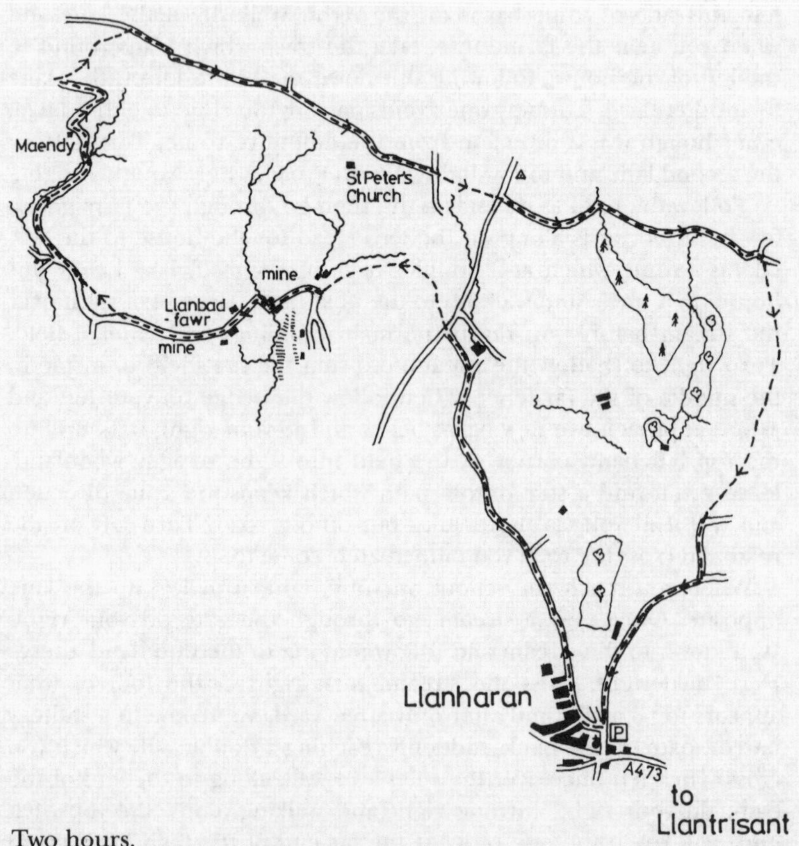

Two hours.

A walk on lanes, tracks and some paths in open country, along sunken lanes, on humpy ridges, past derelict mine buildings and others whch have been converted to agricultural or allied use, past the very battered remains of St. Peter's Church and with wide views including over the Bristol Channel. Ascents are comparatively gentle and tend to zig-zag up the steeper hillsides, but you need to go up to obtain the views!

From Llantrisant take the A473 signposted Bridgend. At the edge of Llanharan turn right up the small road which leads off immediately adjacent to the car park by the pub The High Corner. (The A road bends to the left, that to Brynna goes straight ahead.) Park near the church which you come to almost immediately.

Walk on up from the church, turning left pretty soon down Danygraig Road. This presently bends to the right and starts to gently ascend the hillside. Keep on the track till it comes to an end, a gravelled track leading off to the right and a sunken path on ahead. Take the sunken path which is initially hedged and tree lined on each side. Through a gate ahead on the path, the hedges have been removed and you approach and then pass on your right a set of newer farm buildings. When you reach a T-junction shortly beyond these barns, turn right and almost immediately left back on yourself through a gate into a field. Once in the field follow the remains of the wall with its fence on the far side on your right. This will lead you round to a gate into the next field where the path becomes more of a track. Keep to this track as it circles above old mine buildings in the valley to your right, and which then drops down to join the lane which serves these buildings.

Turn right on this and walk between the various old buildings and barns passing in front of the farmhouse beyond. Past this the track turns right and then left to circle the base of the hill on your right. You pass above another old farm and keeping to the main track soon bend further to the right. The track then drops slightly down into some woodland, passing through a gateway as it does so.

Shortly afterwards it splits and you take the right hand fork signed to Maendy Farm. This gradually ascends the hillside following a stream on your left along the edge of some old woodland. The track then crosses the stream and enters the farmyard. Take the first gate out on your right, just past a small range of buildings, and take the track which angles right, up and across the hillside, keeping left at the fork in the tracks which occurs fairly imminently. This track will dog-leg you back round to the left and lead you to a collection of walls and gates. Stay on this side of them all, dog-legging to the right this time and following the track which shadows the wall on your left. Through the gate at the next field boundary turn half right and walk up to the track in front of the far field boundary.

Turn right on this track, which you follow for a reasonable way, though its status keeps changing. Through the first gate it gains a wall on your right, but is unfenced on the left. Beyond a boggy patch on the left you pass through a gate onto a section which is semi-walled and hedged on both sides. It is towards the end of this section that you can see the remains of St. Peter's Church off to your right, and for that matter have some of the best views of the Bristol Channel.

Beyond St. Peter's Church you enter a boggy patch where there is more of a path than a track, but keep on much the same line to the gate at the far end. Through this turn left on the track, then after a few yards right through a gate which leads onto a track. This soon curves to the left into the hillside, and then to the right once more. All the time you stay at much the same level, though once across some streams and overlooking a wooded valley on your right you start to slightly ascend and meet an old stone wall coming up from the valley. You follow this for a few tens of yards till you come to gate through it. Go through this and follow the track up to the right of the summit. Keep right at the first and second forks so that you follow a track-cum-path which shadows the wooded valley on your right, and gradually drops downhill. This will lead you to a gate at the bottom onto a narrow tarmacced path. Turn right onto this and it will widen in stages to become a major lane which will lead you back to the church where you parked.

MARGAM ABBEY

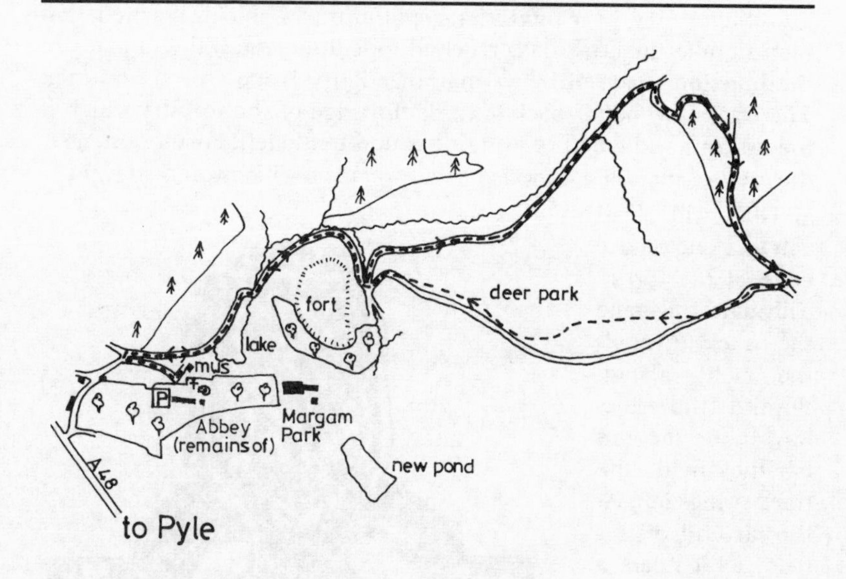

One and three-quarter hours.

Set in rolling bracken and rhododendron covered hillside through Margam Country Park's deer park, with views over Port Talbot to the sea and Gower. At the start of the walk lie Margam Abbey, now a parish church but formerly a Cistercian Abbey, along with a museum of standing stones, and a café. The walk is almost all on main tracks.

Leave the M4 at junction 38 and take the A48 to Pyle. However, almost immediately beyond the roundabout at the motorway junction turn left onto a little road signposted to Margam Abbey and Museum. Follow this road round to the right and park by the church.

Walk back down the road for a couple of hundred yards, then take the road off to the right almost back on yourself. This will lead you to a lake and here take the track to the right which leads along the lake shore. At the end of the lake the track turns right and then left across the feeder stream. Then follow the stream on your left, keeping on the main track which later bends right and uphill to the saddle between the hillfort to your right and a gentler rise to your left.

In this saddle you join a major track on which you turn left. This leads you along a valley on your left and towards some forestry. Once into the forestry, bear right at the split in tracks quickly reached, and then right at the crossroads reached soon after. You will find many of the junctions marked by waymarking signs of one type or another. The track now bends back towards the edge of the forestry which it follows for a while before swinging round to the left. Further on, near the crest of the hill, it meets another track, on which you turn right.

This will lead you to a gate on the edge of the forest. Through this take the track through the field ahead. Beyond the gateway at the far end of the field the track swings left. At the far end of this field, as it nears a stone wall, you turn right down a grassy sunken lane and this will lead you to a metal ladder over a stone wall.

The true path veers slightly to the right of the track across the grass, but keep to the track if you wish. Once you meet the track at the foot of the hillfort, turn right and take the second left to retrace your steps back to the abbey.

Notes on Margam Abbey

The current buildings date from the latter half of the twelfth century, but a Celtic church stood on the site previously. In 1147 the earl of Gloucester granted the French Cistercian Abbey of Clairvaulx all the land between the rivers Arfan and Kenfrig, some 7,200 hectares, to found a daughter house. As with all Cistercian abbeys this was dedicated to St. Mary.

It soon grew with grants of land, and at its peak had some 38 monks and 48 lay brothers, the latter working the abbey's own farm and some shallow coal mines. The abbey owned land as far as Grangetown in Cardiff, in Bristol and the Vale of Glamorgan. Its ships traded with Bristol and the west country; in 1291 the abbey owned 5,000 sheep and also had the right of wreck of sea along the nearby coast.

However, life was not always prosperous. The numerous wars between the English and the Welsh constantly saw losses in their sheep flock, losses sometimes added to by disease. Sand blown from the nearby dunes buried buildings and covered some of the best land, and on occasion the abbey had to be granted the tithes from neighbouring churches to help it survive and meet its requirements for hospitality. On one of these occasions it had to provide for King John and his army on his way to Ireland. Perhaps it was during this time that it came to know the king for it was the only contemporary authority to accuse John of the murder of his nephew, Arthur. The abbey was always recognized as a seat of learning and power, and the copy of the Domesday Survey held by the British Museum is that produced at the abbey.

By the time of the dissolution the complement of monks had reduced to just 9, but the land holding had expanded to 20,000 hectares. Less than half of the abbey's nave was retained for use as a village church, but by the 1800's even this was falling into disrepair. The Talbots, descendants of the purchasers at the dissolution, repaired the building, lowering the roof, adding extra windows and raising the buttresses and topping them with Italianate camponiles.

Ex-almshouses still stand by the church, and the school building has been converted into a museum of stones—largely Celtic crosses from the surrounding area, but also a Roman milestone re-used as a Christian memorial, and mediaeval grave slabs, including that of Robert, Abbot of Rievaulx in Yorkshire, who died at Margam in 1307.

AFAN ARGOED

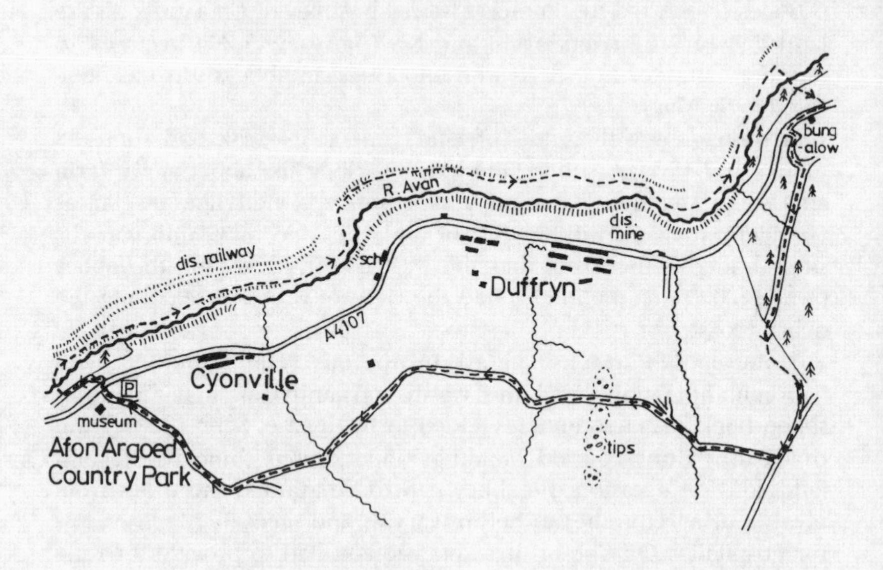

Two hours.

A pleasant walk along the Afon Afan and in the woods and hills above Duffryn, passing through its coal tips. Mainly on tracks, with one very short section of A road. No major ascents, though there are some short and very sharp ones and with one awkward river crossing—a footbridge turns out to be either very large stepping stones or at higher water a combination of a pipe, metal planks and concrete. Especially after recent heavy rain, take great care. There is a miners' museum and café where the walk starts and ends.

Park at the car park at Afon Argoed Country Park just west of Duffryn and Cynonville on the A4107.

Cross the A road and follow the track zig-zaging down to the river, crossing the cycle track made from the disused railway, and then the river itself by the bridge provided—in this instance a very good one.

Over the river bear right on the track which is marked by pink and white banded posts and which shadows the river. Further along the waymarked path leads left up the bank and you want to take this, to join another disused railway line on which you turn right. Beyond paths off to the left to ruined farm buildings and roughly opposite the eastern end of Duffryn village, bear right through a small gate on a blue waymarked path. This shadows the old railway line, but closer to the river, eventually becoming more of a track and leading out onto a lane at the nearside of a football pitch. Turn right on the lane and cross the river by the stepping stones or makeshift bridge. Pass through the gate at the far side and turn half-left up a path up the bank—taking the steeper of the two options offered. Just to the right at the top the fence is partly altered to allow walkers to cross. Over the fence turn left and leave by the exit onto the road.

Turn right on the road and after a hundred yards or so take the signposted track uphill into the wood on the left. At the split in the track, take the right hand less well used but also waymarked track, and follow this up the hill, crossing two forestry routes on the way. The track then swings round near the edge of the woodland before leaving the wood by a gate.

Follow the track on the far side, it in turn shadowing a fence and the remains of a wall on your right, and slowly turning to the left, then right. Pass through one gate and at the junction of tracks near the valley bottom, turn right along the hillside. At the split in the track across the next stream, take the left hand track which then climbs across the hill and passes between the tips. Beyond these you cross another stream and keep following the hillside, the track curving first right and then gradually round to the left to cross another stream. Beyond another short ascent once over this stream another track meets yours at an angle from the left. Not far ahead the track then meets a gate on the right through which you go to follow the sunken track back down to the car park, miners' museum and café.

Notes on Mining History

The Welsh coalfield is sandwiched between the Old Red Sandstone of the Brecon Beacons, and the plateau of the Vale of Glamorgan. The coalfield itself is a basin and where the stratas of coal measures reach the surface at the periphery, the valleys are more open and less restricted. These were also the easy areas and therefore the first areas to be mined, where coal could be quarried or extracted from shallow pits. The better coal, however, lay in deeper seams.

Mining dates back to the Romans who found gold and lead. The Cistercian monks and the Normans extracted coal, lead and iron from outcrops near the surface, but it was not till the Act of Union under Henry VIII that the demand for coal started to expand.

Originally most fire for extracting and forging metal was provided by charcoal, and with heavily oak-wooded valleys timber for charcoal production was plentiful. But with Henry's and then Elizabeth's demands for brass and iron for cannon, demand rapidly increased and as timber became scarcer and harder to find, so began a switch to coal. By 1600 it was even being exported.

Coal mining really took off with the iron industry. In a belt from Hirwaun to Blaenavon lies rock containing all the ingredients for iron production—limestone, iron stone and coal, plus plentiful water to power mills and provide cooling. Manpower also provided no problem as the growth of the industry coincided with an agricultural recession and a population explosion, and people from central and north Wales, the English Midlands and Ireland moved in, often forming their own separate village communities.

The need to transport the iron increased the demand for canals and railways, the latter providing yet another stimulus for the iron industry. This coal boom was to last from 1850 to 1920.

To the south the ports also expanded. Newport handled the bituminous coal for locomotives; Cardiff, Penarth and Barry the 'Best Admiralty' coal, smokeless fuel for the Royal Navy and the French navy. In the west the ports handled anthracite, as well as other products of mines and industry such as copper, nickel and tin plate. Industrial development spread out from the Merthyr Tydfil area to the Rhondda, and mines sprouted up and down the valleys as entrepreneurs looked for better and often deeper coal.

To raise this coal to the surface a water balance was devised. An empty tram in which the coal was brought to the surface, was filled with water at ground level, the weight being more than its equivalent filled with coal waiting at the bottom of the shaft. In pits which weren't free draining this system caused horrendous working conditions as water swilled around. As the pits went deeper and further into the hillsides, so came a need for ventillation. This was provided by lighting a fire at the bottom of a shaft, the updraught causing air to be pulled down a nearby second shaft. However, the fires caused methane to explode, causing mayhem in many mines. In 1842 children as young as five and a half were opening and closing the doors in the shafts which controlled the flow of air, whilst older children filled or even pulled the drams. The general conditions, especially the dust, caused disease, stunted growth and physical deformities.

In 1862 an act of Parliament was passed whereby all mines had to have two separate shafts for increased safety, and very gradually conditions improved with mechanical ventillation and more and safer machinery.

Above ground the mining families lived in houses which often consisted of just one room down, with 5 or 6 sleeping in the one upstairs room. The garden was shared with a pig and chickens. There were virtually no sewers or drains; the roads were unmade and the fresh water was usually taken by industry. Again, conditions gradually improved under a number of public health acts.

From the 1920's the problem of working in the mines with its associated ill health and danger, became balanced by one of unemployment. The strike for better pay in 1926 led to the brief General Strike, after which the miners felt betrayed as their own strike continued. Then came the recession in the 1930's, ended by the start of the Second World War, but since then there has been a steady replacement of coal by oil and even nuclear power, and continuing concerns over coal fire pollution. Imports of cheaper, cleaner fuel from vast open cast mines, or shallow ones worked by cheap labour, have also hit the industry hard.

During this retrenchment period the effects of mining continued to batter communities. In October 1966 a tip above Aberfan slid onto the village swamping the primary school and killing over a hundred children. This prompted a massive clean up of the valleys, with tips being removed or made safe and landscaped. Since then, the mines themselves have been closing at a fast pace, and now the valley sides are a mixture of natural slope and gentle landscaped tip with concrete drains to take water away from potentially unstable waste, whilst gaps appear in the villages below as mine buildings are demolished.

PONTYCYMER

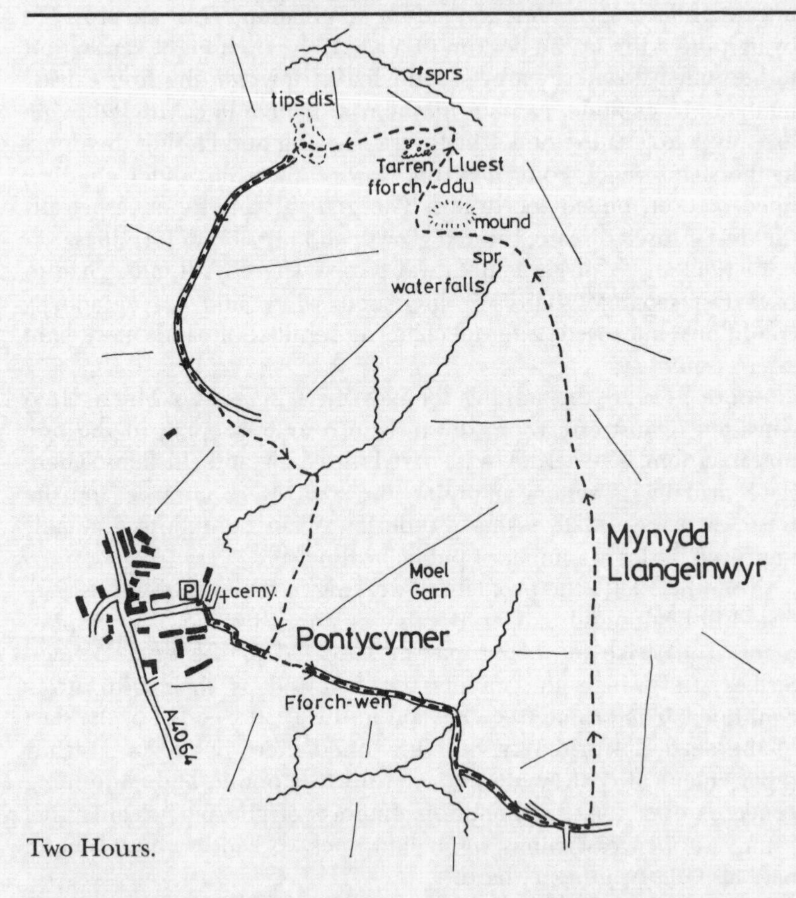

Two Hours.

This route is over rolling hilltop as well as shadowing fields clustering around the edges of the hills. There are tumbling streams and wide ranging views. The walk is on a mixture of tracks and paths.

Take the A4064 into Pontycymer almost to the end of the line of shops, turning right up Alexandra Road just before a bend to the right. Go all the way up this road and park at the top by the cemetery.

About three houses down from the cemetery on the right of the road as you drove up it is a small pathway. Walk along this, cross the top of a lane leading downhill, then at the fork immediately ahead, bear left and up the side of the cemetery. At the top corner with the cemetery the path bends to the right and follows the fences on your right, soon becoming a track. Just keep walking in much the same line and the track follows field boundaries on your right and leads round into a little cwm over the shoulder of the hill. Here you still follow field boundaries on your right, and soon pass just above Fforch-wen farm. You leave the farm down a track which crosses a stream and which then bends to the right and further on once more to the left.

It then climbs up the hillside following the cwm's head on your right and comes out in a saddle in the hill. Here you turn to the left, passing just to the left of the highest placed electricity pylon and where you should find a sheep path. This soon joins a more major track which leads you uphill to the left of the highest parts of the hill.

Later, on your left, you look down on to an area of boulders called Moel Garn. If at any stage on this part of the walk you are unsure of the line in which you should be travelling, as the path does revert to being more a sheep track, keep heading in the general direction of the radio mast way ahead on the hill top.

Once you've passed above the head of the next stream, the path swings to the left passing round a mound on the hillside. Swing round the mound (here the path almost disappears for a while) and once on the far side drop gently down the hillside to the first stream which flows from it. As you reach this you should come to a more obvious path which turns left more steeply down the hill and passes at the foot of a stony outcrop called Tarren Lluest-fforch-ddu. As you leave this behind you look out for the stile over the fence above the old mine workings. Cross this and then the path crosses a limb of the old mine before once more semi-disappearing into long grass on the far side. Round the corner of the hill you drop down slightly onto an old tramway immediately above the mine workings, and walk along this, bearing right when it makes a split ahead.

As you swing round the hillside you come close to some stone walls on your right marking the upper limits of fields. When at the closest place to the walls, you take a path off to the right and shadow the fields down the hillside, passing above a lane and car parking area, then crossing a stream and walking up the path on the far side. At the corner of some walls you cross the stone stile and the path now follows some rather overgrown field boundaries on your right till it rejoins your original route as you reach a fence ahead. Here you turn right and retrace your steps.

YNYSHIR

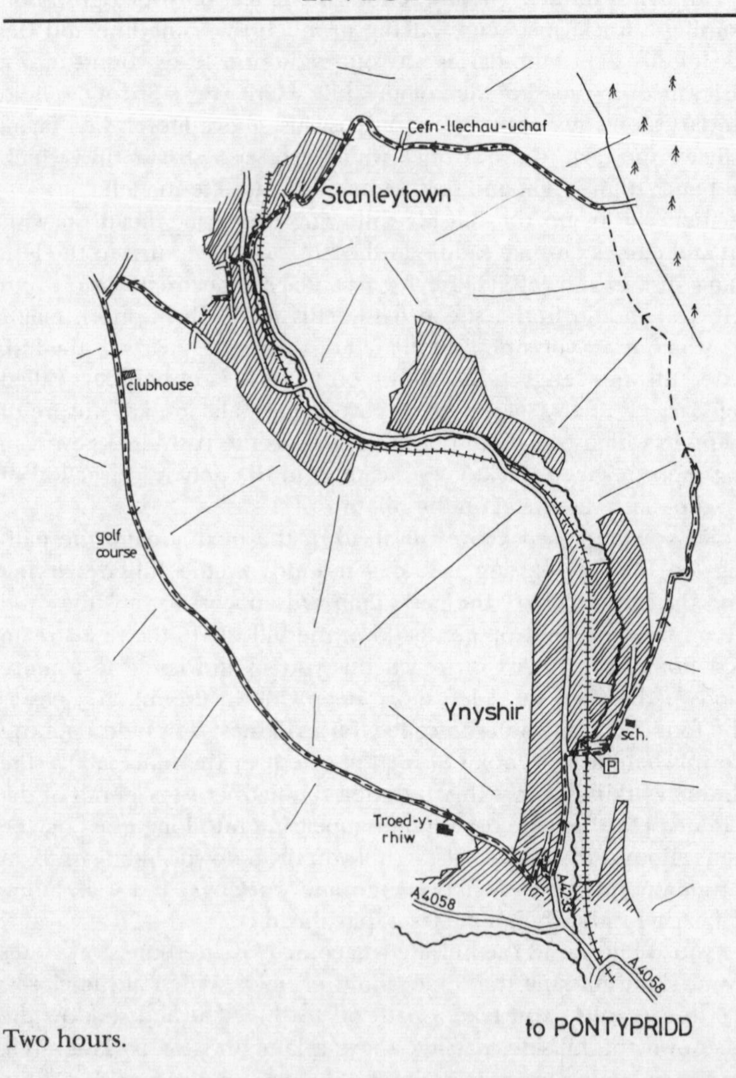

Two hours.

A walk largely on tracks on open hillside, through a ridge top golf course, and with wide views—the valleys with their older villages, the middle slopes with the newer estates. There are two longish but never too steep ascents, and similar and opposite descents.

From Pontypridd take the A4058 to Porth, then bear right on the A4233 Rhondda road. As you leave Porth look out for signs to the Ynyshir Industrial Estate, essentially the first road right out of the centre of Porth, and turn down this where you can park.

Walk on down the road, bearing left and up past the school. The road turns into a track at the end of the houses and then continues slanting up and across the hillside. As it nears the crest it becomes more of a path and almost fades away. When you reach a gate in the fence on your right and a great belt of conifer woodland is staring you in the face, turn almost left and walk slightly away from the woodland to a gateway where a track further along the hillside meets the next fence over. Through the gateway turn right on the track and this will lead you to a junction with another track near the next corner of woodland. Turn left on this second track and follow it round and then down the hillside, on the near side of a tip, to a farm. The track bends to the right round the farm and becomes a lane, soon making a hairpin turn left and slanting down the hillside into the valley.

As you near the houses you meet a flurry of junctions. Turn left at the first two and right at the third, and the road will lead you down and across a bridge over the river. Turn left on the road over the bridge and almost immediately right up a bank—there are steps out onto the road at the top right hand corner. Turn left on the road and where it bends to the left and downhill, turn right through the gap in the houes and walk up to the next bank. This time climb this to the top left hand corner, a path leading out by the side of a garage. Then turn right and left up past a row of garages. This track soon loses its metalled surface and climbs across the hillside to a junction with another track. Turn right on this and follow it across the hillside, bearing left as it makes a fork and follow it to a corner of concrete wall on your left. Turn left here and follow the wall to the next corner. Here you will join a road serving the golf course, on which you turn left. Just keep to this road, and later track, to and through the golf course, at the far end of which you leave by a gate. The track then gently drops down to a fence on your right, soon to become a more obvious track. Just keep to this down the hillside, eventually passing to the left of a farm. Beyond this you join a fairly steeply dropping street. Take the second road to the left, just past a playground on your right, and then bear sharp right on the first road right. This will lead you back to the A4233, on which you turn left to return to where you parked.

CASTELLAU

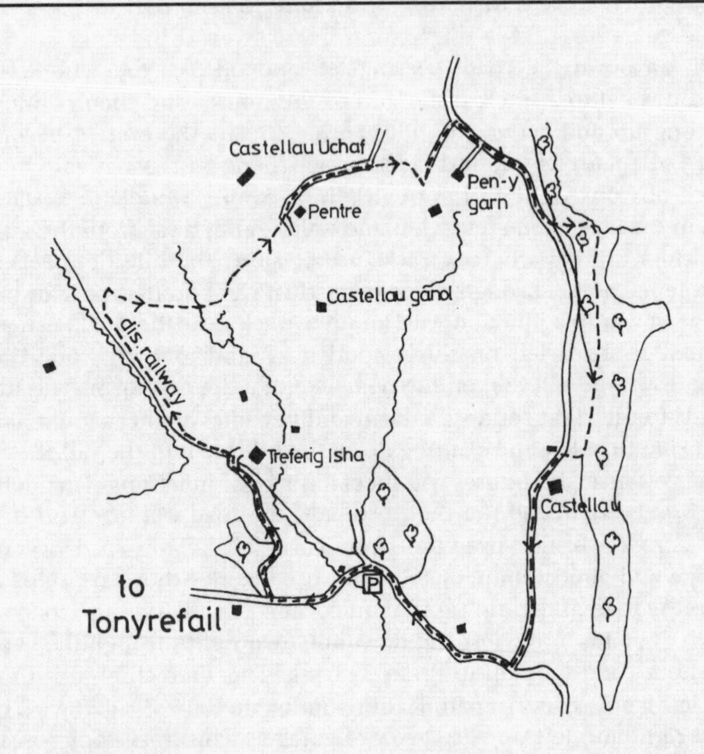

One and half hours.

A walk on minor roads (much of them very minor), tracks, a disused railway line, through ancient fields where paths aren't even visible, through bluebell and deciduous woodland and by streams in fairly gently undulating countryside. There are two slightly awkward fence crossings. At one the fence is fairly pliable, at the other the height can be reduced if you are prepared to clamber up a bank by an ash tree!

At the roundabout between Talbot Green and Llantrisant take the A4119 to Tonyrefail. At the roundabout about a mile further on turn right to the industrial estates. Immediately past the Royal Mint on the left take the unsignposted road to the left. (It may, if the factory is still thriving, be signposted Lacre PDE.) This road curves round the back of the Royal Mint and in about three-quarters of a mile enters Rhiwfelin. At the minor crossroads with the entrance to Rhiwfelin Hospital, turn right. Follow this road past a new trout fishing enterprise to a bridge near some houses, which is the best area to find somewhere to park.

Walk back up the road, ignoring the first signed footpath, till you come to a gateway on the right also signposted as a public path, which leads on to a track to Treferig Isha. (If you reach another farm on the road on the left, you know you've gone a couple of hundred yards too far.)

Walk up this track, which soon bends right and then left. Keep to the track and it will lead you across a stone bridge over the little river. You will then almost immediately come to a stile on your left. Cross this and walk along the path alongside and on the disused railway line. Eventually the woods will thin on your right, a time when you need to start to keep your eyes open. About 150 yards before the line of tall pylons crosses the old railway line you will just about be able to spot the remains of the piers of a footbridge across the river on your left. To your right a probably pretty overgrown short path will lead to some rails into the field on your right. Cross these and enter the field.

Wherever you do cross into the field, walk up to the line of trees opposite which marks the line of an old hedgerow. Once through this head to the far side of the next field just to the right of where the line of small pylons heads out of the field. Here you have to cross a stream and the pliable fence.

Over this head to the top left hand corner of the little field you're in and you'll walk through a gap into the next field. Keep to the wall and fence on your right initially, then cross to the top left hand corner of the field, passing back under the line of small pylons. Here you have the ash tree fence to cross.

Once over, keep to the left of the ruined farm buildings and walk down the old track which leads away from them on the far side, this gradually swinging to the right. You eventually come to a short gravelled section once through a gate, and take the gate at the end of this. The track-cum-path here crosses the next field diagonally and in the field beyond heads towards the farm. Technically the path goes down to the farm and leaves by its drive, but I believe in disturbing people as little as possible, and a better less obstructed route is to turn left once you join a concreted track in this field, and follow it up to the road.

Turn right on the road. Past the old derelict building on your right watch out for the second field boundary running away from you on your left. The first is a wall, the second is a fence. Just past the second go through the gate on your left, and walk down the fence into the wood. The path swings to the right and enters a bracken and bluebell clearing. You have to fight your way a bit to the bottom corner of the clearing and then take the path down to a fence above the stream. Follow this fence—don't worry the path presently improves—and shortly beyond where the fence keeps almost to the stream, the path becomes larger and slopes back up across the hillside eventually emerging into a field. Keep to the edge of the woodland on your left and when you approach a stone wall running up the hillside, turn right up along this, crossing a tongue of field to leave by a gate back onto the road.

Turn left on this and follow it down to a T-junction beyond. Turn right here to return to your vehicle.

CAERPHILLY

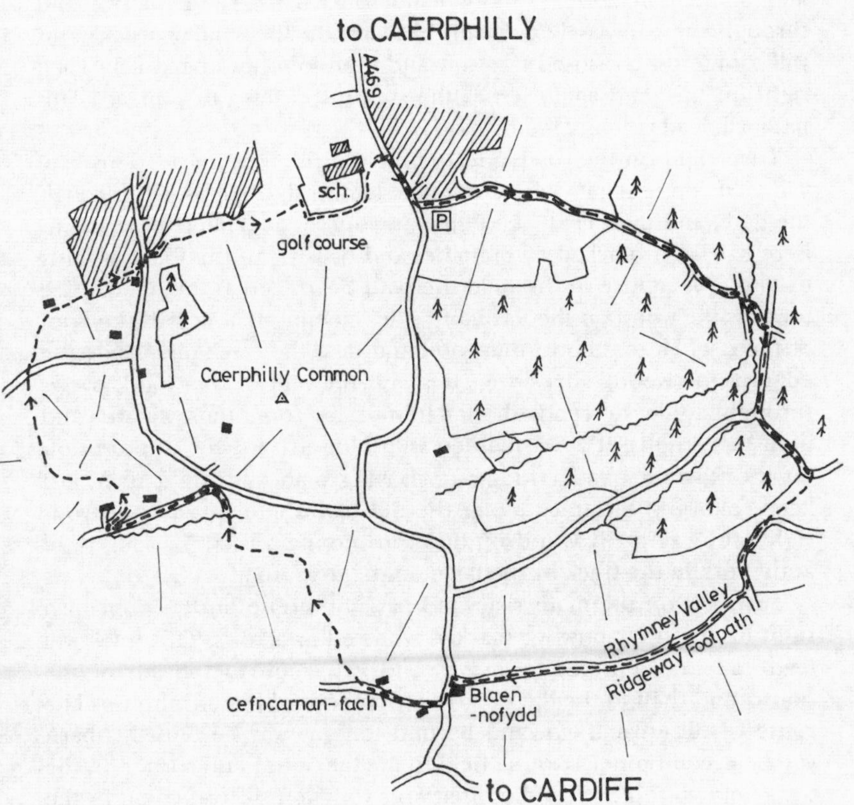

One and three-quarter hours.

A very pleasant walk largely on tracks or well marked paths in rolling mixed woodland and open hillside to the south of Caerphilly. Part of the walk is along the Rhymney Valley Ridgeway which is rich in mid to late spring flowers. There is one slightly awkward fence to cross.

In Caerphilly follow the signs to Cardiff on the A469. Cross the railway line and keep on the road ahead, pass the police station on the left and carry on till you come to two roads off to the left in quick succession. Turn left up the second of these, Warren Drive, and park in the road.

Continue walking along the road, passing out by the kissing gate into the field at the end. Follow the track on ahead along the field boundary on your left and into the woodland beyond. Keep to the track and it will join another more major one. Turn right on this and through the gateway just ahead, bear left on the smaller track. This will soon cross a disused tramway and then joins another track. Turn right on this, and again left at the split just a few yards ahead. This path will lead you to a minor road.

Turn right on the road, and then left at the fork ahead. This lane will lead you to a gate where the lane almost disappears. Go through the gate, and then cross the fence on your right. The actual gateway here has been blocked by branches and brush, but the fence is fairly easy to cross. Once in the field the path heads across the open space towards the wood on the left hand side, meeting it almost at the crest of the rise. Here go into the wood and take the track just inside the edge of the wood. This swings left with the end of the wood, passes through a gate, descends the far hillside for some tens of yards and then turns right. It is waymarked with blue arrows, for you are now on the Rhymney Valley Ridgeway. Having made the right turn, just keep following the track along the old banks and quarries on your right and eventually you drop down to the main road, bearing right at the fork in the track by the farm on the main road.

Turn left on the main road and past the house on the right turn right up the track now waymarked with yellow arrows. This track will lead you into another farmyard, and you keep to the left of the house, and then to the left of a new barn beyond the farmhouse. The route is still waymarked, and beyond the gateway beyond this barn you bear half-right across the field to the far right hand corner. In the next field you follow the boundary on your left till you come to the next gateway, the path then leading across the lower left hand corner of this field and through another gateway, then on in the same line to a stile onto the bracken covered hillside ahead. Here the path turns straight up the hillside, turning left once at the top. Walk along the hill and as you approach the fence ahead, the path turns to the right and descends the hill, later becoming a track and leading you onto a minor road near a road junction with a slightly more main road.

Here we leave the ridgeway for a while and turn left on the road. When you reach some woodland on the left and are near some houses on your right, turn sharp right almost back on yourself on a track which soon becomes a path. This will curve round to the left and soon come to a junction with the ridgeway. Turn left here and the well-worn path takes you round the side of the hill to another road.

Cross this to the kissing gate semi-opposite. In the field turn half-right and leave it by the old gateway just below a clump of bushes and trees. Then head to the burnt out farm beyond, passing just to the right of the old farmhouse and into another field. Follow the hedge on your left towards the houses at the far side, turning left and right through gates here onto the road which services the houses. Walk along this, crossing over at the junction beyond and then on more road and then track to the next road. Cross this and turn left, turning right over the old stone stile you soon come to. This will lead you on a path to the golf course.

Here the route has had to be adapted to fairway and construction considerations! Keep to the left of the fairway in front of you, crossing it nearer the tee to meet a track over the stream on the far side. Turn left to follow the stream, and on the golf holes beyond (the fairways seem to cross each other, so beware of flying golf balls from all angles) cross the fairways towards the large red brick school building. The footpath on the far side technically goes through the school grounds, but since these are now a myriad of courts and pitches and buildings, it is best to turn right at the fence and follow it round to the golf course's clubhouse and leave by the drive to the clubhouse. On the road beyond, turn right to return to Warren Drive and your vehicle.

A note on Caerphilly Castle

The Romans were the first to fortify the area, but it is the much restored mediaeval castle which now dominates the town with its combination of massive walls and lakes. In Britain, only Windsor Castle covers a greater area.

Essentially the castle of Gilbert de Clare, the 'red' earl of Gloucester, (so-called because of the colour of his hair), the vast majority of the castle was built in four summer building seasons between 1268 and 1271. In the previous few years England had been divided by a civil war between an ageing and untrustworthy Henry III, and a party of barons led by Simon de Montfort. The latter wished to reform the government and, because of the lack of their own numbers, had turned to the lesser knights and gentry for support. De Clare had originally supported de Montfort, fighting at Lewes in Sussex. But as the barons' own support gradually waned—England was not yet ready to see its king shackled by other institutions—de Clare's support could be less relied upon. When de Montfort made an alliance with Llewelyn of Wales, the traditional enemy of the marcher lord, de Clare finally left de Montfort's cause and took an active part in restoring Henry III to full power.

However, de Clare was concerned to see the breaches in English society caused by the civil war healed, and headed an uprising in London a few years later to ensure former rebels were treated honourably. As part of an overall settlement Llewleyn was recognized as Prince of Wales and feudal lord of the Welsh princes at the Treaty of Montgomery in 1267. But the wording was unclear about the lords of upland Glamorgan—were they responsible to de Clare as lord of Glamorgan, or Llewelyn as Prince of Wales. De Clare decided to enforce what he saw as his rights and the construction of Caerphilly began.

Llewelyn protested and on one occasion some of the timberwork scaffolding and materials were burnt by the Welsh, but the castle building continued. The reins of government were now very much in the hands of Prince Edward, soon to be Edward I, and he was no doubt already formulating his ideas for the conquest of Wales. Caerphilly Castle could only help.

The design of the castle was partly influenced by the experience of the Crusaders, where massive stonework and wide fields of fire had shown their effectiveness, and partly by de Clare's own experience at the siege of Kenilworth Castle. Kenilworth was de Montfort's main residence where his family and followers held out for many months against a vast siege machine. Part of Kenilworth's defences included lakes.

The site chosen for Caerphilly was therefore not a hilltop, but a narrow spit between two streams. These were enlarged and the excavated material heaped up to form the central island and the embankments of the lakes, as the valley was flooded on the southern side. The approaches to the castle were raised and walled. A dam was formed between the lakes and supplied with a mill for water power to allow the castle to grind its own corn in time of siege. The curtain walls and corner towers were built. Then the level of the central island was raised, along with the walls of the inner and middle wards. The whole was designed so that an enemy had to capture several different sections of the castle before they were in complete control, made more difficult as fire from the inner towers could not just reach the outer wards, but outside the whole castle perimeter, constantly threatening a besieger.

Within 5 years of the completion of the majority of the defences, Edward I launched his first campaign against the Welsh, followed 6 years later by that of 1282-83. Thence followed Edward's own castle building at Harlech, Conway, Beaumaris, Caernarvon and elsewhere, making Caerphilly largely redundant.

However, it didn't prevent the extension of the great dam northwards with twin towers being built at each end, the walls themselves having added towers.

With the end of the male line of the de Clares at the Battle of Bannockburn, the estates were split between three daughters, Edward II's favourite Hugh le Despenser the Younger marrying one and coming into possession of Caerphilly. He remodelled the Great Hall.

It was during Edward II's reign that the castle saw some military activity. It was briefly besieged by a local Welsh leader, Llewelyn Bren (formally de Clare's agent) in 1316, and Edward himself passed through when being pursued by his wife Isabella and her consort Roger Mortimer. Both Despenser and Edward were captured near Llantrisant, after a journey to Neath as part of their plans to disperse the royal treasure. Despenser was hanged; Edward forced to abdicate.

BEDWAS

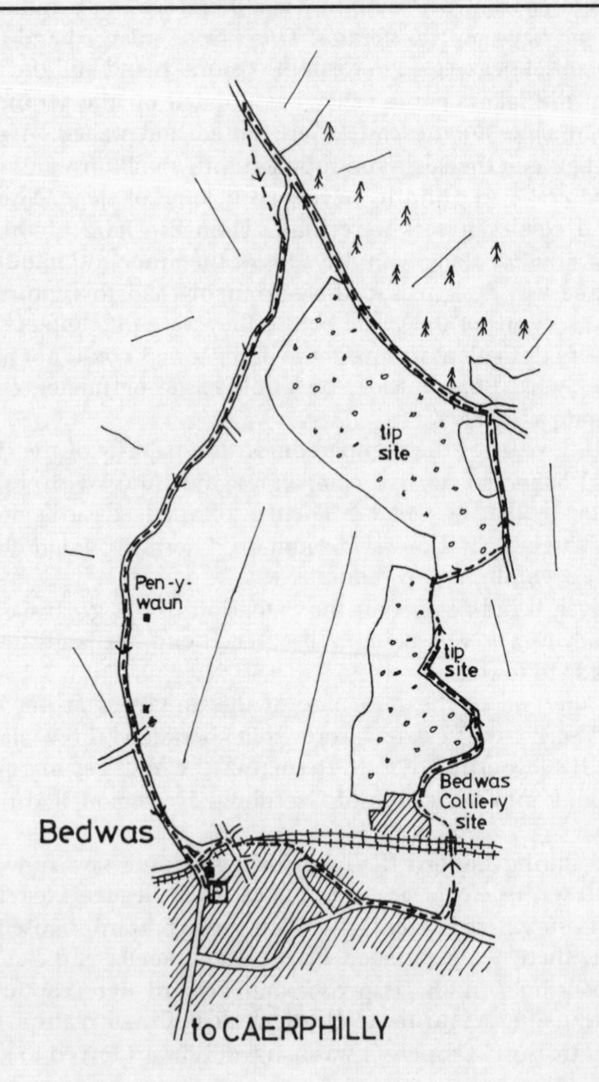

One and a half hours.

A walk past the remains of Bedwas colliery, then along the edge of landscaped tips to the Rhymney Valley Ridgeway path. This is followed for a while before the return is made through farmland. Mainly on tracks and lanes, the walk involves a steady ascent and descent with wide views, including over Caerphilly and its castle.

From Caerphilly take the A468 to Newport. Cross the Rhymney River, just beyond a roundabout on the edge of town, then just past the Bedwas Rugby Football Club on the right, turn left on the little road signposted to Bedwas. Turn almost immediately left again to head straight up the hillside towards the church, parking just before it.

Walk on up the road to the left of the church, bearing right beyond it to keep to the road above the disused railway line. Round the back of the church re-cross the railway line and then turn left onto a track. Take the footpath soon signposted off to the right, to roughly shadow the old line, go behind some houses, cross the top of some open space, then pass between some houses and onto a road.

Turn left on the road, and left again when it joins another road. As you approach more open space on your right, turn left up a track between some houses and walk towards the base of the old Bedwas Colliery. When the track ends take the left hand path up the bank ahead, and cross the old colliery site heading towards the right hand edge of the landscaped waste tips ahead. Here you will find a track which twists and turns till it joins a concrete lane. Bear on up the hill-side on this, it later ending and becoming a stony often semi-sunken but sometimes almost invisible track which roughly keeps to the right hand edge of the tip and carries on up the hillside.

Further up the hill you come to the end of one set of tips and the track bends to the right to pass along the edge of a second set. Keep to this track and it will bend left and lead you to a junction of tracks just in front of some conifer plantation. Here and on the next sections of the walk you will have views into the Sirhonwy valley to the right and the Rhymney valley to the left.

Turn left at the junction and follow the woodland, carrying on for a couple of hundred yards past its far end so you can see more of the view to your right. When the track bends slightly right, turn sharp left almost back on yourself across the hillside. Join the major track which leads away from near the corner of the woodland on your left, turning right onto it and shadowing the old tips on your left.

Just keep to this track around and then down the hillside, it eventually becoming a small road and it will lead you back to the church and your vehicle.

RISCA

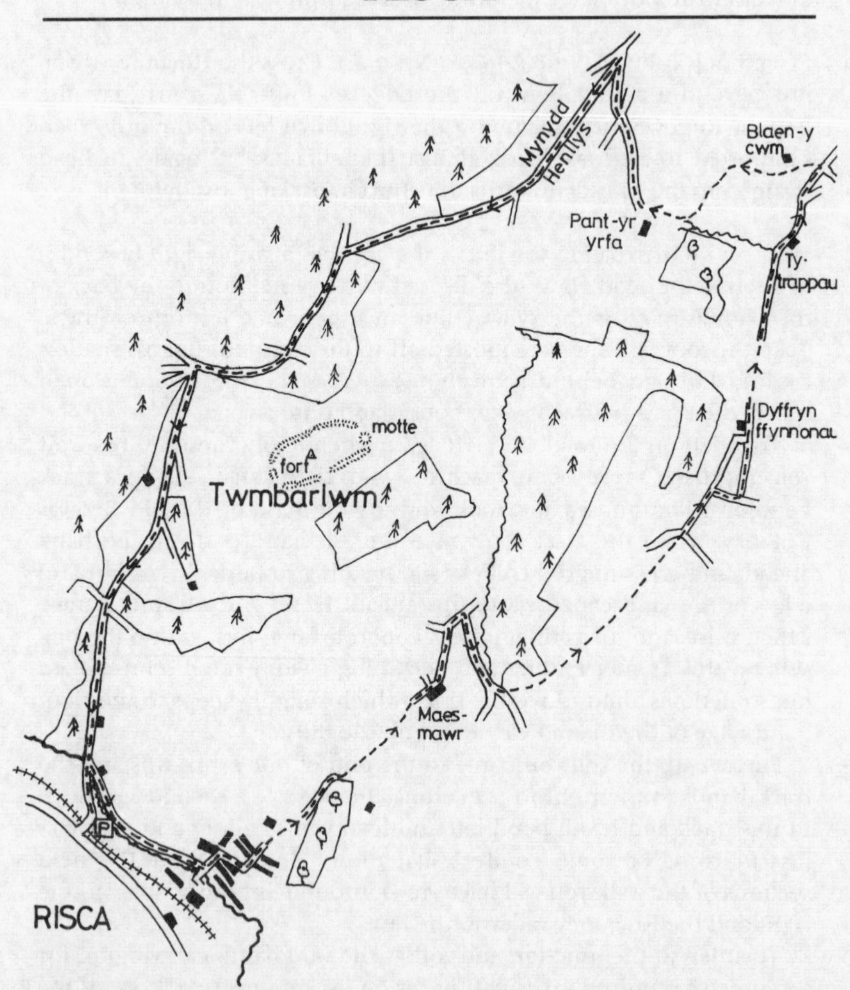

Two and a quarter hours.

On a mixture of tracks, paths and lanes this is a very pleasant walk in rolling countryside. It includes a short section of the Monmouthshire and Brecon Canal and a circuit of the dramatic earthworks of Twmbarlwm with its motte. There is one small but boggy patch for which you need to be prepared.

Take the B4591 (the road that forms junction 27 with the M4) through Risca. If coming from the north, as you pass a cemetery on your left look out for a railway crossing above the road on the left, the turning to which is just beyond a garage. Turn up the road to the crossing and park in the area on the right immediately beyond it. If coming from the south you drive through much of Risca and then look out for a stone church with a spire set back from the road on the right. Not far beyond this is a school on the left, opposite which you turn right this side of a garage. Cross the level crossing shortly ahead and immediately over it park in the area on the right.

Walk on up the road from the level crossing, and soon after it has completed its bend to the right, veer off slightly further right onto a path which will soon lead you along a section of canal. Take the first bridge you come to across the canal, then turn right up the one way street through the houses. This will lead you up to a junction with the road at the top of this group of houses, which you cross and go through the gate in front of a ruined farmhouse.

Follow the track which skirts to the right of the farm and then leads along the top of a stretch of woodland and above a stream, emerging onto a ride. After a few yards on this the path crosses the stream. Bear half right across the next piece of ground, crossing another small stream and entering the field ahead at a corner above this stream. Follow the field edge on your right to the next stile in the far right hand corner. Over this head directly across the next field to another stile, then follow the path which leads round to the left of all the buildings through a rough patch of ground. By the side of one of the stone barns you'll come to another stile which you cross.

Take the track slightly left of straight ahead away from the farm. and when it bends hard left, you carry on half right up the hillside till you join a major track near a gate into a field on your left. Turn right on the track and keep right when it meets a lane.

Follow this lane past the conifer plantation on your left, but near the far edge of this and shortly before the lane starts to bend to the right, take the path which leads left over a broken down piece of fence. This quickly leads to two stiles, one straight ahead, the other in the top left hand corner of a small field. Cross both these and bear to the left of the little causeway on which you find yourself, passing round some springs to a fence below you. Now turn left along this fence and follow it along the hillside, crossing a stile to the left of the line of telegraph poles in a fence ahead, until you come to a lane.

Carry on on this lane along the hillside. When you reach a sunken track leading off to the right, you have a choice of route. The definitive path leads down the sunken way, to bear left in front of the first field boundary and enter the farmyard ahead. However, as the sunken part is comparatively obstructed you could just carry on along the lane you're on and enter the farmyard, turning downhill when you do so. Either way, once in the farmyard walk through it, keeping the farmhouse to your left and the barns to your right, and enter the field beyond. Here keep on much the same line to shadow the bottom of the wood on your left and you'll come to a gate. Go through this and follow the field boundaries on your right to the next house, which you pass to its left and then join its drive.

Walk down the drive, crosssing one stream and turning left through a gate immediately before the second smaller stream. Walk up the field boundary on your right to the stile ahead. Over this turn left and once you reach a big tree almost on the path not many yards ahead, bear half-right on a small path up and across the hillside. This will lead you above a small cwm on your left and to a fence on your right which you follow. The path shadows a stream on your left, then turns to cross it and then comes to a stile. Cross this and walk on alongside the next stream on your left till you come to a gate to a path on which you cross it.

In the field beyond, follow the fence on your right to a gate in the far top corner. Go through this and cross the boggy patch beyond, still following the fence on your right. This will lead you round to the rear of a farm. Keep to the fence on the right and you'll come to the farm's access track leading half-right. Take this, angling across and up the field beyond. Through the gate on the far side continue on the track to the top of the ridge, where you turn left on a major track. As you walk along this make sure you are on the one which follows the crest, almost aiming directly at the motte, and not one which soon slants off to the left.

However further on, the main track does itself bear slightly left, but you turn half-right onto a smaller track which quickly leads to the edge of the woodland on your right. Follow the track down the woodland and enter it at the indented corner you reach. Turn left on the lane beyond and follow this along and then round the hillside till you come to a junction of lanes and tracks. Turn hard left here and cross the very posh stile back out onto the hillside. Take the track which slants right, down the hillside and this will lead you onto a lane which will bring you back out above where you parked.

CAERLEON

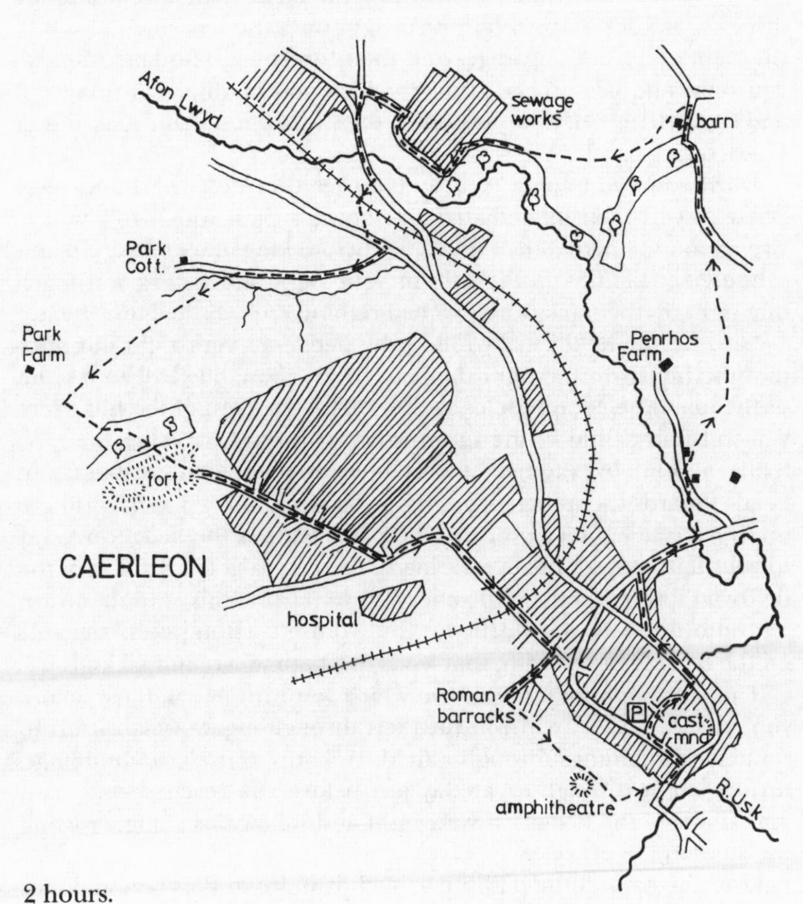

2 hours.

A walk which includes some of the remains of the Roman city of Isca, some open country with wide views, woodland and, less interesting though adding variety, some of the newer streets of Caerleon and the local sewage works! On a mixture of lanes, tracks and paths.

If you keep heading round the one way system in Caerleon, past the remains of the walls of the old castle you will come to a sign to the Roman Baths and you can park in a car park here.

Walk back down the one way system turning left at the pub, Ye Olde Bull, you come to on the first corner. Follow this lane through the houses, bearing left when you come to a T-junction and left again when you reach the main road. Cross the main road and past a line of newer houses on your left, turn right onto a track which passes to the right of a bank of garages and their forecourt. This lane will lead you onto another access road on which you continue, turning left and immediately right at its end to then walk on a main road out of Caerleon.

Fairly soon you come to a bridge over the Afon Lwyd and once across it you turn immediately left down a path which follows the river. Soon the path joins a track and before long, once you are below a house set slightly up the hill on your right and before you reach one right on the track, you turn half-right to cross a stile into a field.

Once in the field intially follow the hedge on your right but once past the house on the right the path heads about 80 yards to the left of the line of telegraph poles as they breast the crest of the hill. Here you will find a stile in the fence which you cross, crossing the next fence beyond by another stile. The path then turns half-left and heads towards the next fence, where you need to keep a sharpish eye out for the stile. Once over this the path shadows the hedgerow away to your left, only gradually nearing it. As you reach the far side of the field you'll spot another stile ahead of you. Cross this, and then turn left onto the path on which you find yourself. (Don't cross the stile on the far side of the path, that leads to a path we are not taking!)

The path soon joins a track on which you turn left and just before you reach a minor road you turn left through a gate which leads to some farm buildings through a field. Walk up to the farm buildings, turning right through a gateway just before you reach them. Then walk down to the hedge on your right and follow this along, crossing two stiles in the process.

Over the second the path turns slightly more to the right and cuts off a corner of the field to your left, leaving the field by a pair of stiles and a bridge on the far side. Here the path heads to the right of the wood which runs along the left hand side of the field, aiming for the far corner of the field.

Here you come to the sewage works, the path leading all around their outside, a recent diversion taking you away to their left on a track. Beyond the works you join a lane and at the crossroads ahead you turn left, then left again on the main road.

Over the bridge not far ahead, and as you reach a line of cottages, the path turns right through a gateway and heads towards the railway line, crossing it by a pair of kissing gates. Once in the field beyond the line, the path swings left round the steep bank, but stays above the bottom corner of the field, and passes out onto the road on the far side via a stile a few yards to the right of the gate. Turn left on the road and very soon right onto a track.

Follow this track but keep an eye out for hedgerows running uphill away from you on your right. Just beyond the second one, and as you start to approach a red brick house, you turn left through a gateway and immediately right through another, crossing the small stream in the valley floor at the same time. The path now follows this stream on your right, crossing into the next field by a stile. In this field the path starts to diverge slightly from the stream, again crossing into the next field by a stile. Cross the third field on the same line, keeping well to the left of the farm on your right. As you near the far hedge, the path turns left and shadows it, entering the wood ahead via a stile. Here you may find you are in a paintball arena, so beware! In the wood the path initially bears to the left for a handful of yards before bearing right uphill through an assortment of semi-camouflaged hideouts. As it nears the crest of the hill it passes through the ramparts of a hill-fort, then rounds an old farm on your right, passes in front of a couple of pigsties, then bears left and onto a lane.

This leads you to a road on which you turn right and walk down-hill. When you reach the main road at the bottom you turn left, and keep on it as it bends to the right ahead as it passes round the hospital. Once over the railway line, take the second road to the right. Walk along this to its end, turning left in front of the school and scout hut onto the path which leads past the remains of the Roman Barracks on your left. (You can enter these by a gate at their corner ahead). Cross the road you reach and over the stile on the far side walk down the rough ground, this time with the amphitheatre remains on your right. The path bends round the bottom of the old wall on your left, then heads across to the far right hand corner of the field. Leave by the stile and turn left on the main road, and left again at the first junction to return to your vehicle.

LLANGYBI

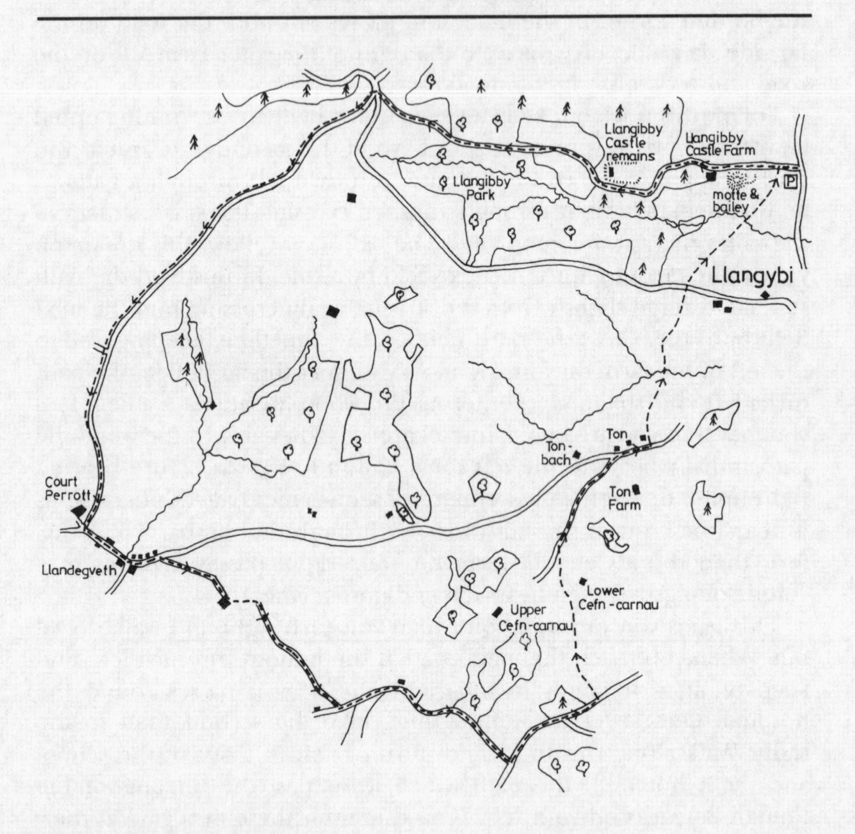

Two and a half hours.

A walk in pleasantly rolling countryside on a mixture of paths, tracks and minor road, most of it quiet but one fairly short section slightly more busy. Fairly extensive views, whilst the walk passes an old motte and the remains of Llangibby Castle.

Just to the north of Llangybi proper on the Usk to Caerleon minor road, and just to the south of the roadside sign informing you you're entering the village, there is a private drive to the west with a GPO letter box on the roadside and a footpath sign pointing to Coed-y-paen. This is where the walk starts and you want to park near here.

Walk up the driveway which soon passes through Llangibby Castle Farm after passing the motte on the left. Through the farmyard the track initially keeps to the right hand edge of the woodland with fields to your right and further on a barn off to the left. As it fully enters the wood it swings left and you keep to the left hand fork soon reached. This will lead you round the remains of Llangibby Castle, of which you might see a few glimpses of stonework, more especially in the winter months. Towards the rear of the castle again keep to the left hand fork which will lead down the side of a hedgerow between two fields, and then swings slightly left in the second field to a gate and back into some wodland.

Once again keep to the left hand fork soon reached and the track will lead you through the woodland and out at the far side. The track swings gently across the field at the end, but is a bit indistinct. If not sure, just aim for the far right hand corner of the field. Here you cross a road, technically going through the gate on the right of the track as the definitive footpath follows the track itself on the headlands of the fields above it. Which you actually take I leave to you—the legally correct route is along the edges of the fields and many of the stiles at field boundaries are fine, some are not. However, further on the track becomes very narrow and more of a stream in winter. If you stay with the fields, a goodly way further on you will leave a field at a T-junction where two tracks meet. The footpath enters the field immediately opposite and continues following the main track through one more field boundary, shortly after which it leads out to the track.

Keep on the track down past a farm, bearing left and left again at the junctions at the bottom. In the village of Llandegveth bear left at the road junction and then almost opposite the last house on the left, turn right up a track. When you reach the entrance to the driveway proper of the house that this track serves, cross over the stile on your left and follow the fence round on your right till you are adjacent to the far end of the buildings. Here turn half-left and walk across to the far left hand corner of the field, passing through the right of the two gates. Head almost straight across the next field, aiming for a point where a hedgerow meets that opposite at right angles from the far side. As you near this you'll see a stile embedded in the hedge on the left of the hedgerow junction. Cross this and then follow the hedge now on your right, crossing a small outcrop of the field at the far side to leave it by a gate above a cottage. Walk down to the side of the cottage, and then out onto the road by its access track.

Turn left on the road and follow it all the way to a T-junction ahead. Turn left here and keep on past a road off to the right. Not far beyond the end of the wood on your left a signpost indicates a path across another embedded stile. Take this, passing through the hedge on the far side of the field by the gateway just up from the corner and head across the second field to near the far left hand corner. Cross the stile here and then turn half right and head just to the left of the farm up the hillside. Cross over the stile into the field above the farm and head up to the top right hand corner. Here pass through the gate on the right and follow the clear track through the field to leave it at the top.

Turn right on the lane and follow it along to the road. Turn right on the road and very soon after two cottages set back and at an angle to the road on the left, and opposite where a footpath sign points off to the right, pass through a gate on the left. Follow the track in the field round the top of the cwm and then turn slightly right to leave the field by the gate ahead. Through this shadow the hedge on your right down to a footbridge. Across this keep very marginally to the left of the line in which the footbridge points and walk up the rise to a stile. Over this you have to cross round a boggy stream and then follow the hedge on your right up to another road.

Cross this, taking a few steps to the right down the road to do so, and take a stile into the field on the far side. Follow the hedge on your right to a short ride, then down the ride to a bridge across a stream. Once in the field on the far side, follow the hedge and fence on your left round the edge of the field, and then turning half-left through the gate in the far corner of the field cross a narrow strip of land back to the drive to Llangibby Castle Farm. Turn right to return to your vehicle.

THE MONMOUTHSHIRE & BRECON CANAL

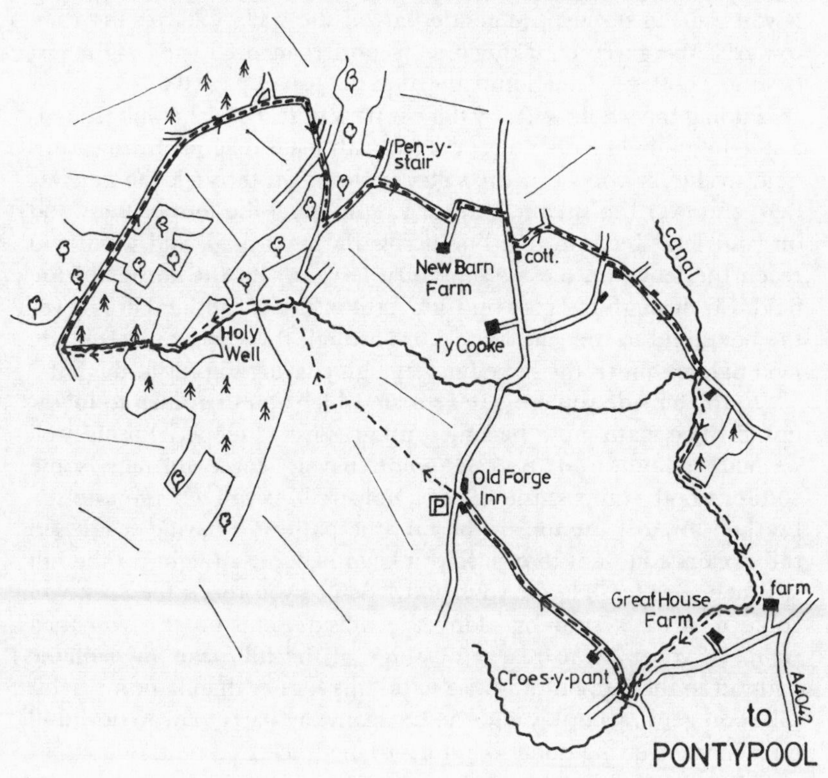

Two hours, though this depends somewhat on your speed of ascent!

This walk consists of two very unequal halves. One includes a steep but lovely ascent of the ridge to the west, through beechwoods and by streams and with far reaching views. Most of this part is on good paths or well worn tracks. The other part is on minor roads and the canal path and is pretty flat. It starts and ends at the Old Forge Inn, which has real ale and food on offer.

From Pontypool take the A4042 to Abergavenny and after a few miles take the minor road left to Mamhilad. Drive along this road for a bit over a mile till you reach the Old Forge Inn on your right. From Abergavenny, take the A4042 to Pontypool, turning right at the far end of Llanover to Pencroesoped. This time the inn will be reached after about 2 miles on your left.

If you want to do just the gentle part of the walk, walk up the road towards Abergavenny, taking the second road off to the right just beyond a cottage. Then jump ahead to the top of page 63.

If doing the whole walk, by the car park in front of the pub there is a stile into a field. Cross this and the path leads diagonally down this field to the far corner in the valley bottom. Go through the gateway here and over the stream, and turn right along the foot of the wood on your left. Keep on that line across the next field, and when you reach the fence on the far side, turn left up it to the corner of the field. Go through the gate on your right in the corner and cross over the next field to the gate opposite. Through this carry on across the next field on much the same line, though curving slightly to the left.

On the far side you cross the stream which you then turn to follow uphill. The path now becomes progressively steeper, but is well waymarked and trod. At one point, having come through some conifer wood, you pass the site of a holy well. As you emerge into the bracken towards the top of the hill, the path now having re-crossed the stream, you want to ensure you keep heading straight up the hill as much as is feasible for your body! Before you reach the crest you come to a track running along the hillside, and on this you turn right. (If you want to reach the ridge of the hill, take any suitable path off to the left, but it is wise to do this sooner than later for fields will soon get in your way and the track anyway starts to drop downhill once more! Having done so, return to the track.)

Follow the track along and gently down the hillside till you pass through a gateway into the edge of some woodland. Through this gate keep on the right hand sunken track and it will lead you round the edge of the woodland and then to a new stoned track. Cross this and bear half right down another sunken track. This will eventually lead you to a semi-crossroads of paths and tracks on the edge of some more open woodland, and you turn left and carry on downhill.

This will bring you onto a lane near a house, on which you turn right and left to walk downhill. This itself joins another lane and you turn left, whence it bends right and leads down to the road. Turn right on the road, then left down another road just before you reach a cottage on the left.

Walk down this road, bearing right and left at the junction with the next road. When you reach the canal, cross the bridge, turn left and walk down to the canal, walking on the tow path back under the bridge. Follow the tow path along, passing under three more bridges before you reach one with a road crossing it. Cross out onto the road by the bridge, cross the canal and turn right at the junction you immediately reach. This road will lead you back to the inn.

A note on the Monmouthshire and Brecon Canal

Originally known as the Brecon and Abergavenny, or Brecknock and Abergavenny Canal, it was built between 1797 and 1812. It was designed by Thomas Daford, junior, who was also engineer of the Monmouthshire Canal. This latter was built to serve the industrial areas from Monmouth southwards, and in part the Brecon canal was built to provide the water for the combined canal system, as both were fed by water taken from the Usk at Brecon.

Apart from providing transport for agricultural produce, the canal also carried other primary produce in the form of stone, coal and iron ore, and there are numerous trackways leading to and from the canal on which horse drawn carriages plied backwards and forwards.

The canal was bought by the owners of the Monmouthsire in 1865, so ensuring their water supply, and the whole was acquired by the Great Western Railway in 1880. Hence it passed into state ownership on the railways' nationalisation in 1948.

By 1970 it had been completely restored by the British Waterways Board and the county councils through whose territory it passes, and is now known as the Monmouthshire and Brecon, even though the vast majority of its now isolated length of just over 33 miles is the old Brecon canal. At Pantymoile it joins the derelict Monmouthshire Canal which, less than two miles away disappears down an 8 foot diameter pipe at the Crown Bridge, Sebastopol.

The whole length of the canal lies in the Brecon Beacons National Park and, with little new development along its length, is considered by those in the know to be about the most scenic of all canal routes in Britain.

THE BIG PIT, BLAENAVON

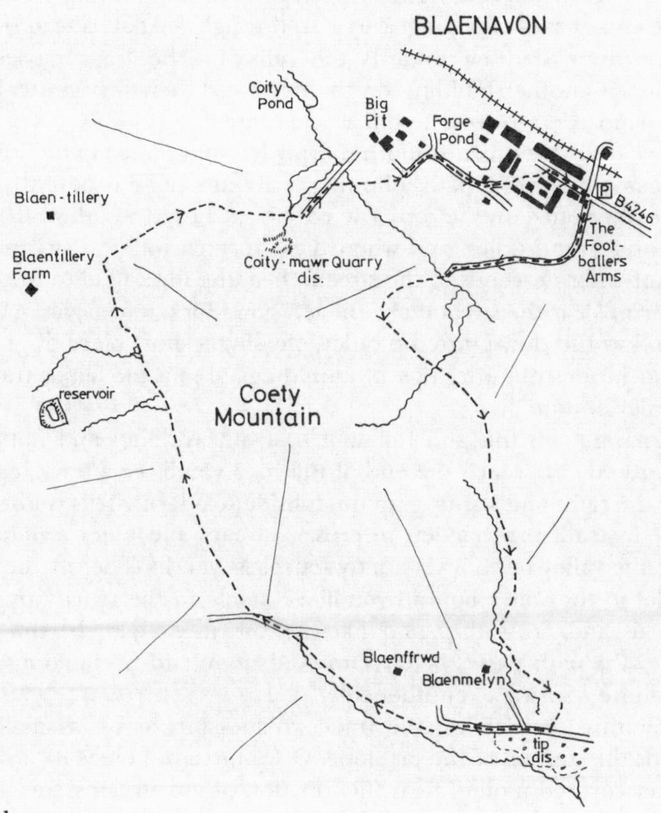

Two hours.

This walk passes above the Big Pit and some of its associated workings, as well as visiting other disused mining sites and crossing open moorland with views over both mining and farming communities. Largely on paths, with some tracks and open hillside with patches of bog. An ascent and descent to and from the moorland is involved, but both are relatively gradual, apart from part of the descent.

Head out of Blaenavon on the B4246 to Pontypool and at the edge of the settlement turn hard right on the road signposted to Forgeside, driving along it till you come to the Footballers Arms on the left, where you can park.

Take the track which leads up the side of the pub towards the hillside, this track bending right in front of some old mining buildings. At the end of these buildings carry on through the gate ahead so that you continue slanting towards the hillside. The track passes the remains of another building on the right and then very gently turns slightly more left to cross an old access route.

Once over this it bends more sharply left and slants up the hillside to become more of a path following a slightly sunken route through the heather once on the top. The path bends right to follow the line of the telegraph poles, and when these in turn follow a stream bed the path later descends to the stream, heading for a field to the right of a farm. Near the stream take the left hand fork, once again a track, and follow this down into the valley, crossing a short piece of ground beyond various old workings and buildings to join the major track in the valley bottom.

Turn right on this and follow it past old workings and flattened waste. As you approach the end of this area you'll see a track leading off to the right and slanting up the hillside to a farm. This is not your route! Instead turn half-left to cross a stream and enter a field just above the valley bottom via a tatty fence. As you look across the field parallel to the valley bottom you'll see a stile in the fence opposite. Head to and cross this, and likewise the next field. In the field beyond the path passes below some old stone and tin buildings and then above a spring to another stile.

Over this turn left on the track which slants across a small rise towards the summit of the far slope. On your right here you can see a heather covered mound near the junction of two streams; this marks the site of a trial mining shaft. When the track bends left near a dip in the ridge, carry on ahead on a path which leads straight on gently crossing the ridge. You have to keep your eyes open to follow the path which is fairly obstructed by heather—but it's slightly sunken, leads in a pretty straight line and is partially marked by tufts of boggy grass.

As you approach the top of the slope down into the valley on your left, you pass above two sets of springs either side of a small headland and look down on a reservoir. Not too far beyond this point you start to leave a bit of a bank on your right and descend into a saddle in the ridge. Keep your eyes open for a two wheeled track which you meet, a few hundred yards before you would be both parrallel to a stone wall on your left and reach the near side of the saddle's bottom. Turn right on this track which will lead you across the saddle and out above the Big Pit. As the track bends right along the hillside, you need to strike off straight ahead across country, before turning slightly right and angling down the hillside. As everything comes into view below you, you want to aim for a gate near the road half way down the hillside. When you reach the road, descend the bank on the far side and walk between it and the fence on your left to the base of an old quarry. When you are immediately above a causeway which aims directly at the Big Pit, clamber down the bank and follow this causeway.

When you reach a boggy stream crossing this route, turn half-right and pick a way round the bogs, aiming for the corner of the fence near the edge of the pit. At this corner, turn left down the fence, crossing the stile near the gate ahead, onto a road. Follow this road round to the right and down to the houses, taking whatever roads through them you fancy to return to your vehicle.

DARRAN VALLEY

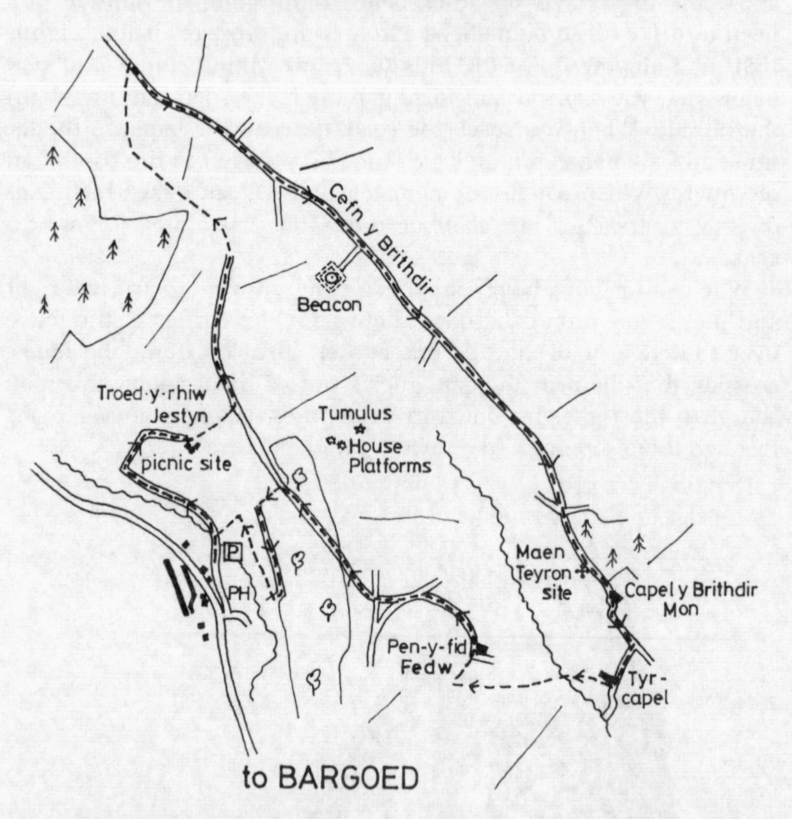

One and three-quarter hours.

A walk on lanes, tracks and paths, passing weirs, a waterfall, through old sessile oak woodland and on pleasant bilberry-clad hillside. You pass an old chapel site and there are wide views. Most of the ascent is gentle, though there is one shortish and sharp section.

From Bargoed drive north on the A469 to turn left under the railway viaduct on the edge of the town on the road to Parc Cwm Darran. Turn left on the next bend following the signs to the Parc. The road makes an S bend through Deri, and you turn right just before the Bargoed Arms on your right and drive down to a car park .

Walk on up the lane from the car park, passing the weirs and make a diversion off to a picnic site on the right to see a waterfall and pool. Back on the lane, bear right at the junction on the track signposted to Troed-y-rhiw Jestyn. The track curves round above the waterfall and up to the farm. Before entering the farmyard you take the stile straight ahead of you and walk straight up beside the fence on your right to the stile on the far side of the field. Once over this bear left along the fence and follow the track which later diverges from the fence and gently swings round and up the hillside. It is a very clear track, only seeming to tend to disappear near the crest of the hill. But here you come to a lane in front of a fence.

Turn right on this, which passes a beacon on your right and then further on becomes gravelled rather than tramacced. The track passes to the right of a small forestry plantation, then passes the old chapel site on the left. Beyond this take the tarmacced lane off to the right at the junction, and adjacent to the farm you reach carry on down the old track ahead for a few yards, to then pass through the kissing gate on your right into the field in front of the farm.

Diagonally cross this field to the bottom far corner and leave it via the bridge and kissing gate. Initially follow the field boundary on your left to the line of old beech trees, then bear half-right to the gate opposite and up the hillside. The line of the path on the ground here has changed to that on the map—and don't worry about the kissing gate in the top corner of the field, that serves another path!

Through the gate turn right and follow the fences and walls round the field, up past the old farm buildings until you reach a gate on your right. Go through this and then follow the wall on your right back down to the farm buildings. Take the old trackway between dilapidated stone walls above the old farm, this swinging you round the hillside to the left. At one point you cross a field where the stone wall on the left has been removed at ground level. This will lead you to a gate back out onto the open hillside. Initially follow the wall on your left and then diverge from it on the track which aims for the radio mast on the hillside opposite. You cross another track, and then yours swings right and down through the sessile oak woodland. Just before a gate into a field at the far end, take the stile on the left. This leads onto a path down the hillside. When it meets a fence ahead it swings left and follows this. Keep to it till you come to gate on your right, through which you go to then cut back across the hillside once more. Over the stile at the far end, turn left steeply down the hillside to another stile to return to your vehicle.

CEFN GELLIGAER

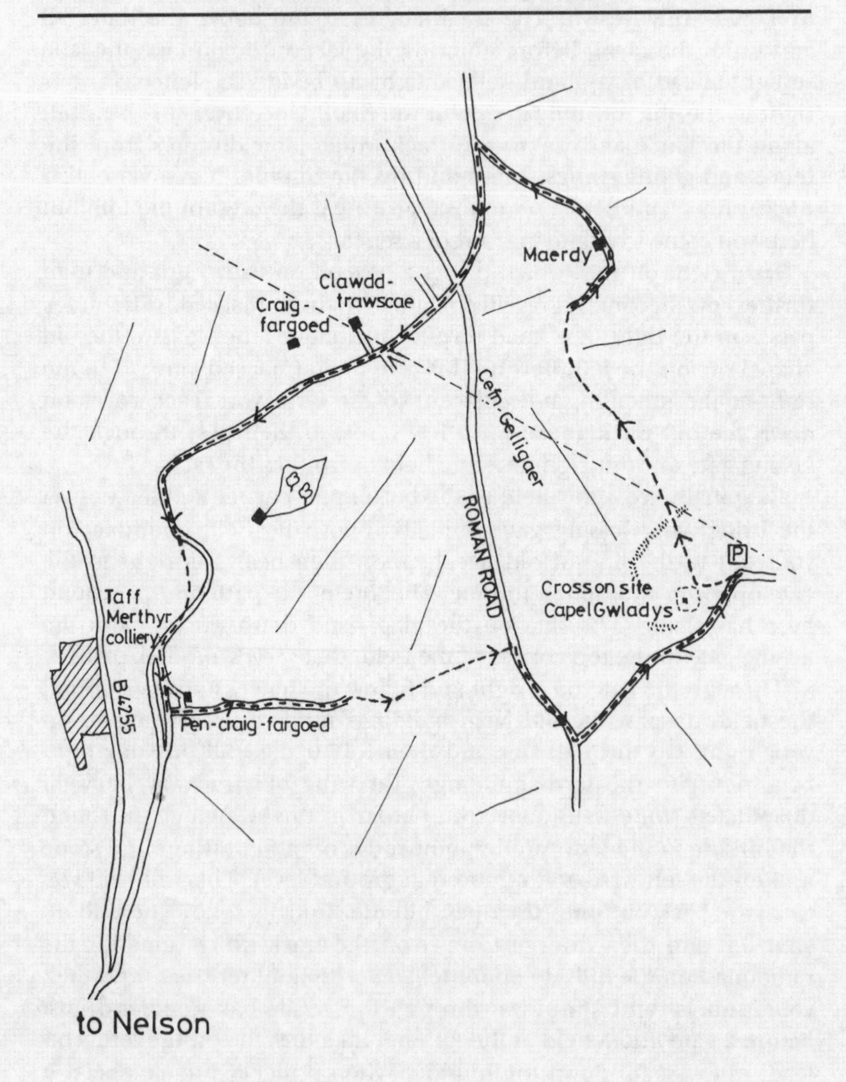

One hour and a half.

A walk on open hillside, partly on minor road though this can be shadowed on the hillside, on tracks and paths, often alongside or between marvellously bulging stone walls. There are all round views and you pass above the still working pit (in 1991) of Taff Merthyr.

From Nelson on the A472 take the B4255 signposted to Bedlinog. Over a little rise in the road turn right onto the B4244 signposted Gelligaer. After about a mile and half, and once you start passing a residential area on the right, take the little road left to Dowlais and Fochrhiw near The Cross Inn. Not far beyond a cattle grid the road splits and you bear right. Keep an eye out for a little cross on the hill-side ahead of you, for you want to park at a point just beyond this where the road makes a bend to the right.

Walk up towards the cross which marks the site of a chapel built in 430A.D. From the cross bear hard right towards the line of telegraph poles, crossing a small earthwork as you near them. There are so many paths and tracks here it is difficult to be precise, but you want to leave the summit of the hill away to your left, but stay above the lower boggy slopes to the right. As you round the hillside you will see the line of a stone wall ahead, and you take the track which heads for a gateway about two-thirds of the way down from the top. Through this turn right and follow the wall towards the right of the farm buildings ahead, turning left as you reach them to pass above some newer barns and then to the right of the house and older barns.

Keep on the farm drive and it will lead you out to a road. Turn left on this up to the crossroads on the summit with another road built on the line of an old Roman road. Cross the crossroads and keep following the road ahead and round to the left as it nears Taff Merthyr Colliery. When the line of the road and the line of some telegraph wires almost meet, at a point where the road bends back into the hillside, take the path which cuts across the indent made by the road. When you rejoin the road, cross it and keep to the track which follows the wall above the road. Go through the gate you reach on the left which leads onto a track up to some derelict farm buildings. The track keeps to the right of all the buildings and further on opens out into a field. Keep to the track ahead (ignore one which leads off right) and this will lead you into another stone walled field which looks like a dead end. However, cross to the far left hand corner and leave by the camouflaged gate. Cross the next field to the right of the wall on the far side, and then head to the gate out onto the road.

You can either turn right and then left on the road to return to your vehicle, or head straight across the hillside via the cross.

CWMDARE

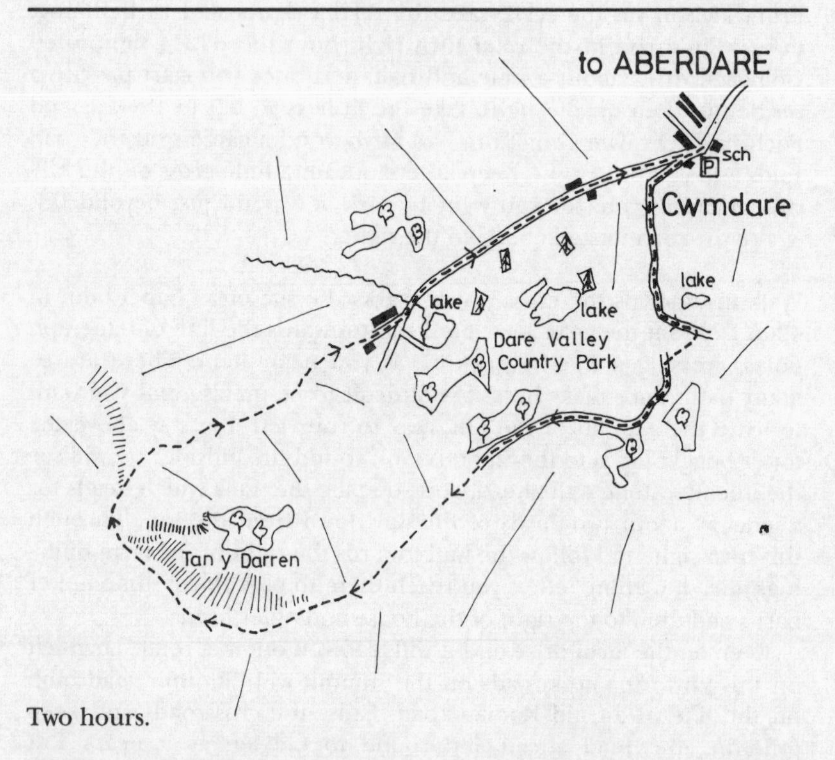

Two hours.

A walk in open countryside passing through the Dare Valley country park and above rocky escarpments. Good all round views and fairly gentle slopes, though the initial up is fairly persistent. Mainly on lanes, tracks and paths.

From Aberdare town centre take the B4275 signposted to Penywaun and Hirwaun. Past the park and towards the edge of the town turn left onto the road signposted to Cwmdare. Park near the crest of the hill by the county primary school.

Walk on along the road, bearing left at the fork quickly reached down Dare Road and where it's signposted to the cascades. Walk on down this road which will bend to the left and lead you into the country park. It climbs uphill beyond the stream and then bends to the left above a lake. Not far after this bend a track leads off to the right and swings up the hillside. Take this and it will lead you round the hillside and steadily uphill above the lakes in the country park. Presently it leads above the rocky crags of Tan y Darren. Here you follow the top of the crags, the track turning to a path and crossing a stream which has its source just to your left. As you start to rise up beyond this stream, you take the path which leads off to the right, curving back down into the Dare Valley.

The path crosses a stile and then gradually drops down the hillside, passing above some hawthorn trees and then round the top of an old quarry beyond which you enter a field through a gate. (Don't take the gate immediately above the quarry.) Here the path bends to the right and drops down towards the farm in the valley bottom, crossing out onto a track and then a lane over a couple of stiles. Once on the lane, bear left at the end of the row of cottages and walk back to where you parked your vehicle.

PONT NEDD FECHAN

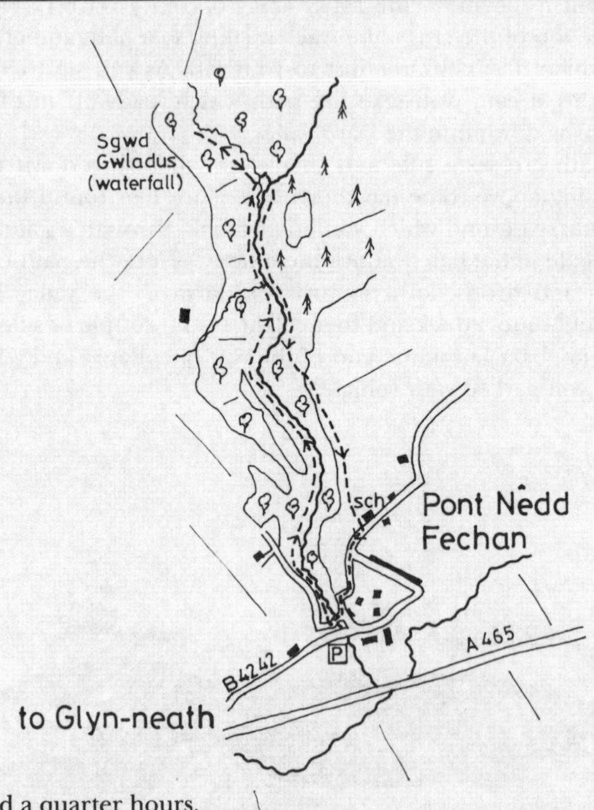

One and a quarter hours.

The circular walk is only for the more adventurous and better equipped with footwear, in that there is a wide stream to ford, itself only fordable with ease in dry periods. Thereafter there are small footpaths to follow along the sides of fairly steep high banks. However, the walk along the river till you need to ford it is on a broad track and you can retrace your footsteps from the waterfall called Sgwd Gwladus with no problems. However, even here decent footwear is needed as the wide path can be quite muddy.

At the junction near the Glyn-neath end of the dual carriageway between Hirwaun and Glyn-neath turn to Onllwyn on the A4109. At the crossroads you reach immediately over the river, turn right and drive into Pont Nedd Fechan. When you reach the Angel Inn on your left, turn left on the little road beyond the inn and park immediately.

Walk on up the road a few yards and turn left in front of the bridge across the river and walk up the wide path along the river bank. You eventually come to a footbridge on your right, but carry on past this to the Sgwd Gwladus waterfall, which is worth a visit. Then return to the footbridge. If you want to tackle the more adventurous walk, you cross the footbridge, otherwise return to your vehicle by the same path.

Over the bridge turn right and immediately ford the stream ahead, so that you end up walking down the other bank of the river which you walked up. The path here is much narrower and passes old mine shafts on your left before coming to the remains of mine buildings. Cross the first stream you come to by these buildings, then turn left to walk up the 'causeway' on its far side. This will lead you past another ruined building and up a ridge of hillside between a gorge on your left etched by the stream you crossed by the river, and a smaller gorge on your right. At the head of the gorge on your right, take a narrow path which leads along the hillside and shadows the river in the valley bottom.

The path undulates and passes through an area of old mine workings beyond which it meets an old grassy track winding its way down to the river. Here you turn left and cross out of the woodland at the top by a stile. The path now follows the fence on your right round the woodland, and when you come to a new fence running away at approximatley right angles to the woodland, you cross this and follow the bracken infested path which then shadows the river valley on your right. You cross other fences but keep on much the same line through fields of bracken till you drop down to another stream as you approach some buildings. Cross the stream and turning slightly to the left follow the boundary on your right, almost immediately crossing a high wooden fence. Keep following the boundary and you come to a stile, over which a short slightly overgrown path leads you past a school and out onto a road.

Turn right on the road and as it bends sharply round to the left ahead, turn right on the signposted footpath just before the bus shelter. This will lead you down a path, with further on many steps, back to where you parked.

GLYNCORRWG

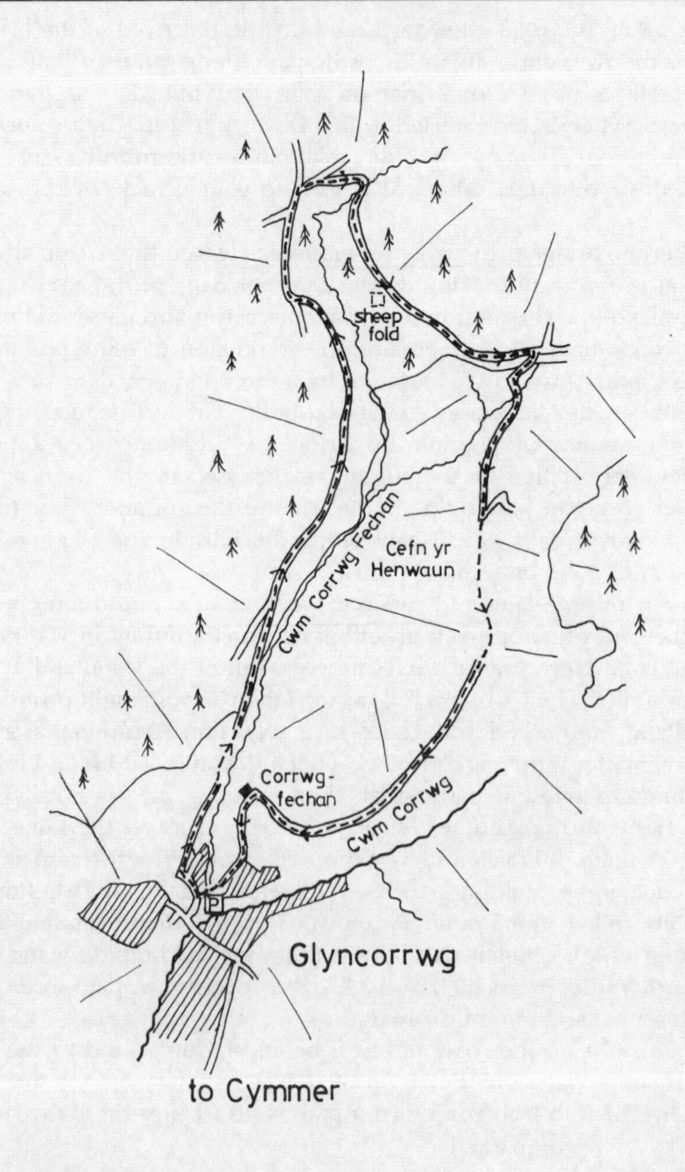

One and a half hours.

A walk partially in conifer forest but even here with glimpses down into a steep stream valley with the sound of waterfalls. Part of the walk is in open country further down this stream, and part follows a pleasant valley with old landscaped mine tips back into the village, over which there are good views. All on tracks.

Park over the bridge in Glyncorrwg, having kept on the main road into the village from Cymer to its south.

Bear right over the bridge and walk up the street called Heol y Derren, turning left after the first small terrace of houses on the left. This track turns right behind the next terrace and leads via a gate onto a gravelled forestry track which winds up to and then through the plantation. Keep to this, and near the top of the valley on your right, bear right at the split in the forestry tracks. This will soon be followed by another split near a broad cleared way through the woodland, and you bear right again. Then very shortly right once more onto a slightly smaller track which soon crosses another stream and starts to wind around the hillside. For a while we leave definitive footpaths as they have been planted over and take alternative tracks, but soon to rejoin the definitive route.

The track passes an old stone sheepfold on the right and further on passes close to the edge of the wood. A few hundred yards beyond this point a short track leads hard right to a gate into a field. Go through the gate, cross the field and follow the track down into the dip before the next hill, part of the hill being a landscaped tip, as are parts of the hills to your left. As you near the dip look out for the track which leads half-left, as you take this and not the one which leads almost straight on up the next hill passing an old railway carriage.

Taking the left hand track, this will lead you round and gently down the hillside before, above Glyncorrwg rising uphill once more. The footpath is shown as crossing fields to the left of the farm you're approaching, to join its drive just below the buildings. However, as this way is obstructed it is best to follow the track to the farm and down the farm's drive back to the village and your vehicle.

RESOLVEN

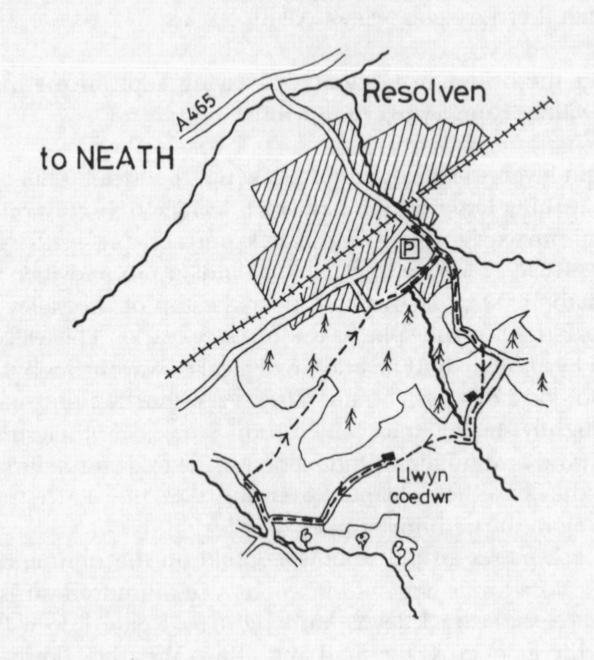

Three-quarters of an hour.

A walk in mixed woodland and fields and passing waterfalls on the lower slopes of the valley, on lanes and tracks. Though a short walk, the initial ascent is fairly steep.

Turn off the A465 Neath to Merthyr road onto the B4434 to Resolven where signposted. Cross the railway line and shortly after when the road bends hard right, turn left onto the road ahead and park near the supermarket almost immediately on your left.

Carry on walking up the road, turning to the right of the Salvation Army building at the fork in the road, and keep on the lane up the hillside and into the woodland. The lane comes to a T-junction with another lane, and here you cross over onto the track which carries on leading up the hillside. Not far along this track you come to a stile on your right which you cross and follow the track slanting across the hillside and past some high wire and then a ruined farm on your right. Beyond this the track curves across a stream and then clambers up into some fields. Carry on walking across the fields and you'll soon come above a farm on your right. Here the track swings down to the farm and passes round to its left, thence carrying on past farm buildings and across the hillside.

You pass a chapel to your right and then meet a lane. Here before you are the waterfalls and it is worth turning left and walking up to the bridge, before making an about turn and walking down the lane. Soon you come to a stile on your left, and though there is a public footpath marked in this area, the path is very overgrown. However if you fancy a brush with vegetation it is worth crossing the stile and following the main path into the ruins of a mine.

The walk itself continues by crossing the stile on the right hand side of the lane as you walked down it, almost opposite the stile just referred to on the left hand side, and situated above a parking or passing area. Here a track leads across some fields and passes out below a farm and then a house. Here it joins a forestry track, but you almost immediately bear left down a path which soon crosses another forestry track. When it leads you out to the top of a tarmacced lane, the path bears right and follows the edge of the woodland, eventually passing above a school and coming out on a lane above the Salvation Army building. Turn left to return to your vehicle.

THE SKIRRID

One and a half hours.

There is a choice of walks here around and over the hill. All have good views, though those from the top are clearly more impressive. The area of the landslip, which local tradition has it took place at the time of the crucifixion, is very rocky and scenic. All the paths are in good condition, though one of the options to or from the Trig Point is very steep and slippery.

In Abergavenny follow the signs to Skenfrith. After passing the T-junction with traffic lights near a garage, close to the centre of the town, go along the straight section of road till near where it starts to rise. Here you turn right. You pass under the main Hereford road, and then over a crossroads where you are on the main road. The road then bends to the left and then the right in a long sweep, beyond which there is a large lay-by on the left with a National Trust sign, and here you park.

At the Abergavenny end of the lay-by is a stile leading to a fenced off path which leads round the fields to the wood at the bottom of the hill. Cross the stile here and follow the path uphill through the wood, later to cross another stile by a wall onto the Skirrid proper. Here you have a choice. Anticipating you probably want to reach the top, take the path to the right, subsequently choosing the options which keep on climbing and this will lead by paths along the ridge and eventually to the trig point.

If you want to come back a different way, you can take the steep path down which curves to the left beyond the trig point and follows the edge of the gorge on your left, eventually picking up a path at the bottom which leads back this side of the part of the hill which fell away. If that is too steep a descent, return along the ridge a couple of hundred yards or so, till you reach a more gentle path leading left and downhill. This will again lead you to the same path near the foot of the enclosed hill land, and you can turn right or left to return to the stile out of the wood. Left will bring you round through the rocks and woods, right through bracken with more views.